16 BIBLE
STUDIES
FOR YOUR SMALL GROUP

16 BIBLE STUDIES

FOR YOUR SMALL GROUP

RYAN LOKKESMOE

BETHANYHOUSE

a division of Baker Publishing Group
Minneapolis, Minnesota

© 2020 by Ryan Lokkesmoe

Published by Bethany House Publishers
11400 Hampshire Avenue South
Bloomington, Minnesota 55438
www.bethanyhouse.com

Bethany House Publishers is a division of
Baker Publishing Group, Grand Rapids, Michigan

Printed in the United States of America

ISBN 978-0-7642-3392-0 (paperback)
ISBN 978-0-7642-3827-7 (casebound)

Scripture quotations are from THE HOLY BIBLE, NEW INTERNATIONAL VERSION®, NIV® Copyright © 1973, 1978, 1984, 2011 by Biblica, Inc.® Used by permission. All rights reserved worldwide.

Scripture quotations identified ESV are from The Holy Bible, English Standard Version® (ESV®), copyright © 2001 by Crossway, a publishing ministry of Good News Publishers. Used by permission. All rights reserved. ESV Text Edition: 2016

Cover design by Dan Pitts

Author represented by Books & Such Literary Agency

22   23   24   25   26   7   6   5   4   3

Contents

Introduction

Ever Deepening

When we open the pages of the Bible, we encounter a rich set of ancient texts that have come down to us, by God's grace, through the centuries. These writings, originally copied by hand and read from scrolls, are now accessed on backlit screens, on mass-produced printed pages, and in audio format. The biblical texts were first composed in ancient Hebrew and Greek but are now available in most modern languages. In the early centuries of the Church, it was a rarity for any person or individual congregation to have a complete copy of the Bible because they were prohibitively expensive to produce and the process of copying and circulating was painstakingly slow. Today, by contrast, many people in the world have instant access to the entirety of Scripture, in their own language, at no cost. It has never been easier to engage with God's Word.

This does not mean, however, that the Bible is easy to engage. Despite having effortless access to the Bible today, many of us struggle to know how to approach it effectively and consistently. While the Bible was becoming more accessible to readers over the centuries because of technology, it was also, in a way, becoming *less* accessible because of the widening gap between our modern culture and the ancient biblical context. As a result, we can easily read the Bible, but the biblical world we encounter in its pages can seem remote or confusing to us. Our ancient Christian brothers and sisters in Christ faced the opposite challenge: The language and cultural context of Scripture was more familiar, but few of them had personal access to a copy of it.

The good news is that with the Holy Spirit's guidance and the help of our brothers and sisters in Christ, we can grow together in our knowledge of and love for Scripture. But we must accept that we will never master the Bible. We cannot hold ourselves to that standard. Reading, understanding, and applying the Bible is an ever-deepening experience, because knowing God is an ever-deepening experience. The author and subject matter of Scripture is God himself. We could never dig deep enough into that topic to find the bottom of it, and we don't have to. God invites us into a personal, perpetually growing relationship with him. He has made himself known to us in the Scriptures, and most fully in the person of Jesus Christ. As the author of Hebrews put it,

> In the past God spoke to our ancestors through the prophets at many times and in various ways, but in these last days he has spoken to us by his Son, whom he appointed heir of all things, and through whom also he made the universe. The Son is the radiance of God's glory and the exact representation of his being, sustaining all things by his powerful word.
>
> Hebrews 1:1–3

This book is a collection of short Bible studies designed to lead you through a meaningful engagement with God's Word. I consider this to be a sequel to my previous book, *Small Groups Made Easy*, which was written to help small-group leaders grow in their practical leadership skills and basic theological knowledge. In this book, as a natural follow-up to the last one, we will dig beneath the subject of small groups to the bedrock below. We will explore the subject of Christian fellowship, which is the main biblical impetus for small groups.

Fellowship is something most Christians would agree is important and biblical, but many would struggle to define it. For some, the idea of fellowship is inspiring and comforting. For others, community with other Christians feels like a nebulous obligation. To the skeptics among us, the notion of Christian fellowship seems like a naïve aspiration. However you may feel about fellowship at the moment, the Bible clearly teaches that followers of Jesus are called into community with each other. Some of God's most precious gifts come only through relationships within the Church.

The term *fellowship* resists a simple definition, but it must be understood if we are to experience its joys. We must look to the collection of specific words used by the New Testament authors in order to gain a sense of it.* You will find that we spend most of our time in the New Testament, especially the letters, because they speak most directly to the subject of Church life.

I've written these studies with the assumption that you will be working through them alongside others in a Bible study or small group, but they certainly can be used for personal study as well. Each chapter will be organized into three sections,

---

*Much of this book is rooted in my study of community-oriented language in the New Testament, including *fellowship* (κοινωνία/*koinōnia*), *one another* (ἀλλήλων/*allēlōn*), *come together/gather* (συνέρχομαι/*synerchomai*), *gather* (συνάγω/*synagō*), and *congregation/church* (ἐκκλησία/*ekklēsia*). The later chapters will explore additional Greek terms with the *syn-* prefix, which are usually translated as *fellow (something)* or *co-(something)*, e.g., *fellow worker* or *co-heir*. More detail will be given on those Greek terms when we reach those chapters.

corresponding to the three basic parts of a small group meeting: Social, Study, and Prayer.

- The **Social** section will include a few memorable icebreaker-type questions designed to deepen personal relationships within your group. One of the questions will serve as a lead-in to the subject matter of the study. If you are not doing these studies in a group, you can use these questions for personal reflection.
- The **Study** section will include Scripture, brief sections of teaching material, and several discussion (or reflection) questions. The questions arise from the biblical text and are usually open-ended.
- The **Prayer** section will include a suggested prayer for the end of the gathering, along with some ideas about how to handle prayer requests.

My hope is that this threefold approach (Social—Study—Prayer) becomes a familiar cadence for your Bible studies, and that you intuitively become familiar with the kinds of questions you should be asking yourself and your group as you prayerfully study the Scriptures.

By the end of these chapters, you will have a cumulative, biblical sense of how Christian community should look and feel. You will discover that Church fellowship is countercultural and often counterintuitive, and it is so much more wonderful than we often imagine it to be. As with the study of Scripture, Christian fellowship is an ever-deepening experience. My prayer is that these studies are helpful and hopeful steps in your journey of faith.

1

Fellowship with God

Social

A few questions to get your gathering started. This can be done during a meal or at the outset of your meeting.

- **Personal question:** If you had to summarize the state of your spiritual life right now, how would you describe it? (Everyone answers.)
- **Open-ended spiritual question:** What's something you feel God is teaching you right now? (A couple people share.)
- **Lead-in question to the subject of the study:** When you think about having fellowship with God, what comes to mind?

Study

Fellowship is one of those words that is familiar to most followers of Christ. We encounter the word in Scripture. Time spent with other believers is routinely referred to as fellowship. Some of our churches even have the word in their name. It's one of those words that is mainly used within the Church, so it generally has a religious connotation. The word fellowship does not appear much in contemporary secular usage unless one is referring to a certain work by J. R. R. Tolkien.

But how should we as people of faith understand this rich term, fellowship? I suspect that for most Christians, the word fellowship refers to the polite company of other Christians.

- How would you define the word fellowship?
- How is fellowship different from other types of social gatherings?

The biblical concept of fellowship is not merely social time spent with other Christians. Fellowship is, after all, an English word and therefore does not appear in the original text of the Bible. The term fellowship is a translation. For the deeper connotation of the word, let's go back to the original language of the New Testament, ancient Greek.

When we read the New Testament and encounter the term fellowship, it is usually a translation of the Greek word *koinōnia*, which appears nineteen times in the New Testament.* *Koinōnia*, at its most basic level, means to have something in common with someone else, or to share something. On a few

---

*κοινωνία; see Acts 2:42; Romans 15:26; 1 Corinthians 1:9; 10:16; 2 Corinthians 6:14; 8:4; 9:13; 13:14; Galatians 2:9; Philippians 1:5; 2:1; 3:10; Philemon 1:6; Hebrews 13:16; 1 John 1:3, 6–7.

occasions in the New Testament, the term refers to literally sharing something by giving a gift or making a financial contribution to a group in need.†

This ancient term, *koinōnia*, has been defined as "a close association involving mutual interests and sharing . . . association, communion, a close relationship."‡ *Koinōnia*, therefore, means to be especially close to someone because you share something with them.

• How does this definition of *koinōnia* deepen your view of what Christian fellowship is?

The most amazing and overlooked aspect of the term *koinōnia* is that it is used to refer to not only our relationships with brothers and sisters in Christ (which is what we usually think of), but also our relationship with God. Because of Christ, the door has been opened for us to experience fellowship—*koinōnia*—with God Almighty. In this chapter, let's explore some of the examples from the New Testament that describe our relationship with God as *koinōnia*. In the passages below, I will display in bold the English word that is a translation of *koinōnia*.

In the opening verses of Paul's first letter to the Corinthians, he writes,

> I always thank my God for you because of his grace given you in Christ Jesus. For in him you have been enriched in every way— with all kinds of speech and with all knowledge—God thus confirming our testimony about Christ among you. Therefore

---

†See Romans 15:26; 2 Corinthians 8:4; 9:13; Hebrews 13:16.

‡Frederick W. Danker, et al., *A Greek-English Lexicon of the New Testament and Other Early Christian Literature* (Chicago: University of Chicago Press, 2000), 552–553.

you do not lack any spiritual gift as you eagerly wait for our Lord Jesus Christ to be revealed. He will also keep you firm to the end, so that you will be blameless on the day of our Lord Jesus Christ. God is faithful, who has called you into **fellowship*** with his Son, Jesus Christ our Lord.

1 Corinthians 1:4–9

- What are these few verses about?
- At the end of this passage, we are invited into fellowship with God's Son. How are we able to experience that fellowship?
- How does the invitation to fellowship relate to what Paul says earlier in the passage?

A little later in the same letter, Paul speaks about the observation of the Lord's Supper as a form of *koinōnia*:

The cup of blessing that we bless, is it not a **participation** in the blood of Christ? The bread that we break, is it not a **participation** in the body of Christ?

1 Corinthians 10:16 ESV

- In what ways do you think observing the Lord's Supper is sharing in or participating in the blood of Christ and the body of Christ?
- Read 1 Corinthians 11:23–26, where Paul quotes Jesus's words about the Lord's Supper. How does this passage help you understand what Paul means by participating in the body and blood of Christ?

---

*Throughout, any emphasis in quoted Scripture passages has been added.

In the final verse of his second letter to the Corinthians, Paul again uses the term *koinōnia*:

> May the grace of the Lord Jesus Christ, and the love of God, and the **fellowship** of the Holy Spirit be with you all.
>
> 2 Corinthians 13:14

- What do you think it means to have *koinōnia* with the Holy Spirit—to be close to him because you share something together?

Read Romans 8:9–17 (ESV):

> You, however, are not in the flesh but in the Spirit, if in fact the Spirit of God dwells in you. Anyone who does not have the Spirit of Christ does not belong to him. But if Christ is in you, although the body is dead because of sin, the Spirit is life because of righteousness. If the Spirit of him who raised Jesus from the dead dwells in you, he who raised Christ Jesus from the dead will also give life to your mortal bodies through his Spirit who dwells in you.
>
> So then, brothers, we are debtors, not to the flesh, to live according to the flesh. For if you live according to the flesh you will die, but if by the Spirit you put to death the deeds of the body, you will live. For all who are led by the Spirit of God are sons of God. For you did not receive the spirit of slavery to fall back into fear, but you have received the Spirit of adoption as sons, by whom we cry, "Abba! Father!" The Spirit himself bears witness with our spirit that we are children of God, and if children, then heirs—heirs of God and fellow heirs with Christ, provided we suffer with him in order that we may also be glorified with him.

- How does this text illuminate what Paul means by fellowship with the Holy Spirit?
- How does knowing that we experience *koinōnia* with the Spirit change your view of God and your relationship with him?

In his letter to the Philippians, Paul explains how this fellowship with the Spirit should affect our mindsets and behavior:

If you have any encouragement from being united with Christ, if any comfort from his love, if any **common sharing** in the Spirit, if any tenderness and compassion, then make my joy complete by being like-minded, having the same love, being one in spirit and of one mind. Do nothing out of selfish ambition or vain conceit. Rather, in humility value others above yourselves, not looking to your own interests but each of you to the interests of the others.

Philippians 2:1–4

- How should *koinōnia* with the Spirit change us, according to Paul?
- Is it possible to live this way without the Spirit changing us from the inside out? Why or why not?

In the same letter, Paul speaks about his own life of faith and about his desire to live in a way that honors Christ. In this text he mentions his desire to experience *koinōnia* in a way that might challenge us:

Whatever were gains to me I now consider loss for the sake of Christ. What is more, I consider everything a loss because of the surpassing worth of knowing Christ Jesus my Lord, for whose sake I have lost all things. I consider them garbage, that I may gain Christ and be found in him, not having a righteousness of my own that comes from the law, but that which is through faith in Christ—the righteousness that comes from God on the basis of faith. I want to know Christ—yes, to know the power of his resurrection and **participation** in his sufferings, becoming like him in his death, and so, somehow, attaining to the resurrection from the dead.

Philippians 3:7–11

- Paul expresses that he wants to know Christ, and that part of that is participating in, sharing in, his sufferings. What do you think that means?

Read Jesus's words in Matthew 16:24–25:

Then Jesus said to his disciples, "Whoever wants to be my disciple must deny themselves and take up their cross and follow me. For whoever wants to save their life will lose it, but whoever loses their life for me will find it."

- How do Jesus's words deepen your understanding of what Paul means in Philippians 3?
- How does suffering or taking up our cross to follow Jesus draw us closer to him?

In this chapter, we have focused on the *koinōnia* we experience with God because of Christ. In the next chapter, we will focus on *koinōnia* with each other. The two concepts are linked in the New Testament: Because God has invited us into fellowship with him through Christ, we are able to have fellowship with each other—not just polite social relationships—but genuine, Spirit-led *koinōnia*. Jesus's disciple John put it this way in his first letter:

We proclaim to you what we have seen and heard, so that you also may have **fellowship** with us. And our **fellowship** is with the Father and with his Son, Jesus Christ.

1 John 1:3

Key Ideas in This Study

- *Koinōnia* is a word that refers to a closeness with some-one because you share something in common.
- Fellowship with God is possible because he has invited us into that relationship.
- Part of our fellowship with Christ is reflecting on the meaning of his sacrifice.
- We have fellowship with God through his indwelling Spirit, which leads us to live a God-honoring life marked by humility and unity with other Christians.
- Part of our fellowship with God is sharing in his suffering, or as Jesus put it, taking up our cross each day.
- Fellowship with each other flows from our fellowship with God.

Prayer

1. Starting with yourself, ask the group for two things:
   - A quick update on any ongoing prayer requests
   - New prayer requests

2. Write down the prayer requests as people share:

3. Ask someone in the group to close your meeting with prayer.

- **Sample prayer:** Lord Jesus, thank you for calling me into fellowship with you. I thank you that fellowship with you is not an abstract concept, but a true, deep, personal relationship. Help me to feel that, Lord, and to seek out true fellowship with my brothers and sisters in Christ. Holy Spirit, help me to sense your indwelling presence, and supernaturally enable me to humbly live in a manner that honors you. Help my fellowship with you, God, to be the catalyst and basis for my other relationships. I trust that you'll do this in me, because I cannot experience true fellowship with you or others apart from your leading. Amen.

2

Fellowship with Each Other

Social

A few questions to get your gathering started. This can be done during a meal or at the outset of your meeting.

- **Personal question:** Give us a quick snapshot of how things have been going since our last meeting—maybe a high and low point. (Everyone answers.)
- **Open-ended spiritual question:** What's something you feel God is teaching you right now? (A couple people share.)
- **Lead-in question to the subject of the study:** If fellowship (*koinōnia*) is a closeness you feel with someone because you share something in common, what are some things that Christians have in common that make biblical fellowship possible?

Study

During the 1930s, the Church in Germany was coping with the snowballing influence of Hitler and the Nazis. Dietrich Bonhoeffer, a German pastor and theologian, saw the ways the Church was being warped by Nazi ideology and used for Hitler's purposes. Bonhoeffer devoted himself to resisting Hitler by supporting the underground Church in Germany. This brave brother in Christ was eventually arrested, imprisoned, and executed for his actions.

In his classic book *Gemeinsames Leben* (*Life Together*), Bonhoeffer reflected on the often-overlooked beauty of Christian fellowship. He wrote,

> It is true, of course, that what is an unspeakable gift of God for the lonely individual is easily disregarded and trodden under foot by those who have the gift every day. It is easily forgotten that the fellowship of Christian brethren is a gift of grace, a gift of the Kingdom of God that any day may be taken from us, that the time that still separates us from utter loneliness may be brief indeed. Therefore, let him who until now has had the privilege of living a common Christian life with other Christians praise God's grace from the bottom of his heart. Let him thank God on his knees and declare: It is grace, nothing but grace, that we are allowed to live in community with Christian brethren.*

- What strikes you about this passage from *Life Together*?
- How has Christian fellowship been a gift of God's grace in your life?

---

*Dietrich Bonhoeffer, *Life Together: The Classic Exploration of Christian Community* (New York, NY: HarperOne, 2009), 20.

- Why do you think it's easy to disregard or take for granted the gift of fellowship with brothers and sisters in Christ?
- How would your life change if Christian fellowship was no longer a possibility for you?
- How might you offer Christian fellowship to someone who is unable to have it because of the circumstances of their life?

The apostle Paul describes the Church with several metaphors in his letters, the most well-known being *the body*. In Romans 12, Paul wrote:

> By the grace given to me I say to everyone among you not to think of himself more highly than he ought to think, but to think with sober judgment, each according to the measure of faith that God has assigned. For as in one body we have many members, and the members do not all have the same function, so we, though many, are one body in Christ, and individually members one of another.
>
> Romans 12:3–5 ESV

- What stood out to you about this text?
- What character quality is Paul describing in the first sentence of this passage? How is this quality a prerequisite for Christ-centered community within the Church?
- Why is it important to remember that God gifts people in the Church differently? What is the risk of forgetting this fact?
- What do you make of Paul's statement that each member of the Church belongs to the others? How should

this shape our expectations about relationships within the Church?

In his letter to the Ephesians, Paul speaks about unity in the body—the Church:

> I therefore, a prisoner for the Lord, urge you to walk in a manner worthy of the calling to which you have been called, with all humility and gentleness, with patience, bearing with one another in love, eager to maintain the unity of the Spirit in the bond of peace. There is one body and one Spirit—just as you were called to the one hope that belongs to your call— one Lord, one faith, one baptism, one God and Father of all, who is over all and through all and in all. But grace was given to each one of us according to the measure of Christ's gift.
>
> Ephesians 4:1–7 ESV

- Paul lists some qualities that Christians must embrace in order to maintain fellowship and unity in the Church. Which of these qualities do you struggle with the most, and why?
- Count the number of times the word *one* appears. What do you think is Paul's main message in these couple of verses?
- Paul explains that Christ has given gifts to his people in whatever ways he sees fit. Do you find this encouraging? Confusing? Frustrating? How does knowing this change your view of God and others?
- Paul began this passage by urging his readers to live a life worthy of the calling they had received. In what ways does living in humble unity lead us to live a life worthy of our calling?

Paul continues to elaborate on the body of Christ in this same chapter of Ephesians:

> Christ himself gave the apostles, the prophets, the evangelists, the pastors and teachers, to equip his people for works of service, so that the body of Christ may be built up until we all reach unity in the faith and in the knowledge of the Son of God and become mature, attaining to the whole measure of the fullness of Christ.
>
> Ephesians 4:11–13

- Here we see a few examples of the ways God has distributed gifts within the Church. What, according to this passage, is God's purpose for gifting these people in the way that he has?
- What do you believe it means for the body of Christ to be built up, and how does this relate to Christians experiencing fellowship together?
- In *Life Together*, Bonhoeffer wrote, "The Christian needs another Christian who speaks God's Word to him. He needs him again and again when he becomes uncertain and discouraged, for by himself he cannot help himself without belying the truth. He needs his brother man as a bearer and proclaimer of the divine word of salvation."* What do you make of what Bonhoeffer said?
- What, according to the Ephesians 4 passage above, are some of God's ultimate purposes for the Church being built up?

*Bonhoeffer, *Life Together*, 23.

Next, Paul explains the results of God building up the Church:

> Then we will no longer be infants, tossed back and forth by the waves, and blown here and there by every wind of teaching and by the cunning and craftiness of people in their deceitful scheming. Instead, speaking the truth in love, we will grow to become in every respect the mature body of him who is the head, that is, Christ. From him the whole body, joined and held together by every supporting ligament, grows and builds itself up in love, as each part does its work.
>
> Ephesians 4:14–16

- According to Paul's words in this passage, what are the risks to the Church if we are not unified and built up together? What do you think it looks like to be a spiritual infant?
- Paul explains how it looks when the Church is unified and building each other up in Christ-centered fellowship. What stands out to you about these verses?
- What does it look like to speak the truth in love, and why is this so important?
- In what ways does the contemporary Church in the Western world confuse or obscure what Paul is describing here?

In Romans 12 and Ephesians 4, we have engaged with this rich metaphor of the Church as a body. In Ephesians 2, Paul uses the metaphor of the body to speak about the Church, but then switches to another metaphor: a temple of the Lord.

In this text, Paul is speaking about how through Christ, a way has been opened up for the Jews and gentiles to become God's people together. The former religious and cultural hostilities that divided Jews from gentiles can—and *should*—cease under the banner of Christ. It is a beautiful picture of how *koinōnia* in the Church transcends racial and social barriers.

> [Christ] himself is our peace, who has made us both one and has broken down in his flesh the dividing wall of hostility by abolishing the law of commandments expressed in ordinances, that he might create in himself one new man in place of the two, so making peace, and might reconcile us both to God in one body through the cross, thereby killing the hostility. And he came and preached peace to you who were far off and peace to those who were near. For through him we both have access in one Spirit to the Father. So then you are no longer strangers and aliens, but you are fellow citizens with the saints and members of the household of God, built on the foundation of the apostles and prophets, Christ Jesus himself being the cornerstone, in whom the whole structure, being joined together, grows into a holy temple in the Lord. In him you also are being built together into a dwelling place for God by the Spirit.
>
> Ephesians 2:14–22 ESV

- What in these verses spoke to you the most?
- What does this tell you about fellowship within the Church?
- Paul begins with the metaphor of a body for the Church and then switches to the metaphor of a house or temple. How do you think the body and temple metaphors are similar, and how are they different? What do they each tell you about the Church?

The Church is meant to experience fellowship with each other—*koinōnia*—in a way that is made possible because of

Christ. The Church is not meant to be a group of Christians trying to be nice to each other. We are meant to experience life in Christ, and life together because of the hope we share in Jesus. We are meant to build each other up in humble unity and reach across social barriers to find our common identity in Christ. The Church is the body, Christ is the head. We are a temple within which his Spirit dwells.

This fellowship we enjoy with each other is made possible by Christ, and Jesus wants to use our fellowship not only for our own growth, but as an example to the world that is watching. As Jesus said in John 13:

> A new command I give you: Love one another. As I have loved you, so you must love one another. By this everyone will know that you are my disciples, if you love one another.
>
> John 13:34–35

Our experience of *koinōnia* in the Church not only enables us to live a life worthy of our calling, but it preaches the gospel to the world. Our love for one another is a testament to Jesus's transformative work in our hearts.

Key Ideas in This Study

- Fellowship with other Christians is a gift of God's grace.
- The body of Christ is made up of people with different gifts.
- To live a life worthy of our calling, we must humbly seek unity within the Church.

- God has gifted leaders and teachers in the Church to build up the Church toward maturity.
- Speaking the truth in love is a marker of spiritual maturity and Christlikeness.
- The Church is also a temple of God, where his Spirit dwells.
- Loving fellowship is a testament to Jesus's transformative work in our hearts.

Prayer

1. Starting with yourself, ask the group for two things:
   - A quick update on any ongoing prayer requests
   - New prayer requests

2. Write down the prayer requests as people share:

3. Ask someone in the group to close your meeting with prayer.

   - **Sample prayer:** Lord Jesus, I want to experience life in the body as you've designed it. I want to know my gifts, appreciate the gifts in others, and humbly seek unity. I want to be built up along with my brothers and sisters in Christ, as we all rely on you to mature us. Help me to know how it sounds to speak the truth in love, and show me how to love your Church the way you do. Amen.

3

Love One Another

Social

A few questions to get your gathering started. This can be done during a meal or at the outset of your meeting.

- **Personal question:** Give us a quick snapshot of how things have been going since our last meeting—maybe a high and low point. (Everyone answers.)
- **Open-ended spiritual question:** What's something you feel God is teaching you right now? (A couple people share.)
- **Lead-in question to the subject of the study:** What do you think it means to love one another within the Church, and what are some obstacles to doing that?

Study

As we read at the end of the previous chapter, Jesus called his followers to love others. If you were to ask people on the street what Jesus's message was, they would probably say the word *love* or the phrase *love each other*—or something like it—in their answer. Most people—whether or not they have ever read the Bible—understand that love and compassion were at the heart of Jesus's message. This is why there is a sense of public indignation when there is a perception that a group of Christians has not loved others well. There is an expectation that Christians are *supposed* to be different and have failed in some way. Christlikeness is expected of Christians, even by those who do not follow Christ.

- What do you think about this public expectation that Christians should be radically loving and compassionate because Jesus was?

But what did Jesus really say about love? What does the New Testament teach about loving others, and how is it even possible to love others in the way Jesus described? Let's review Jesus's words in the Gospel of John. In his final hours with his disciples, on the eve of his arrest, he spoke about love:

> A new command I give you: Love one another. As I have loved you, so you must love one another. By this everyone will know that you are my disciples, if you love one another.
>
> John 13:34–35

Jesus gave the commandment to love and followed it immediately with a description of *how* our love for each other should look. We are called to love each other as Jesus loved us—which raises the profound question:

- How has Jesus loved us?

On the heels of that question, we must ask ourselves:

- How can we love others in a way that reflects how Jesus loved us?

Understanding how Jesus has loved us is the key. Doing this will paint a picture in our hearts of how we are to love others. Jesus also said in these two verses that "everyone will know" that we are his disciples if we love others in this way. This tells us that part of Jesus's purpose in calling us to love each other was to make his message observable to a watching world.

- What message does it send to the world when we love others as Christ loved us?

Jesus loved people who were not easy to love in first-century Galilee and Judea: the sick, those who lorded their wealth over the impoverished, the publicly sinful, tax collectors, gentiles, etc.

- Who in our twenty-first-century world are like these groups, and why have we struggled to love them well?
- Are there individuals in your life whom you have failed to love as Christ loved you? How can you start?
- In what ways have you made it difficult for others to love you well?

A couple chapters later, in John 15, Jesus expounded further on the subject of love:

> This is my commandment, that you love one another as I have loved you. Greater love has no one than this, that someone lay down his life for his friends. You are my friends if you do what I command you. No longer do I call you servants, for the servant does not know what his master is doing; but I have called you friends, for all that I have heard from my Father I have made known to you. You did not choose me, but I chose you and appointed you that you should go and bear fruit and that your fruit should abide, so that whatever you ask the Father in my name, he may give it to you. These things I command you, so that you will love one another.
>
> John 15:12–17 ESV

Jesus alludes to his upcoming crucifixion. The greatest expression of love, as Jesus states here, is self-sacrifice.

- Have you ever been loved by someone else in a way that was sacrificial for them? How did it make you feel?
- How does it look to love others within the Church in a sacrificial way?
- How might it look to love others outside of the Church in a manner that is self-sacrificing?
- How would self-sacrificial love serve as a testimony to who Jesus is?

In the Gospel of Matthew, we read about an interaction Jesus had with the religious authorities. They asked him about the greatest commandment, and he answered with these famous words:

> "Love the Lord your God with all your heart and with all your soul and with all your mind." This is the first and greatest commandment. And the second is like it: "Love your neighbor as yourself." All the Law and the Prophets hang on these two commandments.
>
> Matthew 22:37–40

Loving God with our whole being—emotional, spiritual, intellectual—is the greatest commandment. Following closely on its heels, however, is the second greatest command: to love others as we love ourselves.

- What do you think it means to love others as we love ourselves?
- How is loving others in this way inherently sacrificial?

Jesus also stated that loving God and others fulfills the fundamental call of Scripture: "All the Law and Prophets hang on these two commands," he said. The apostle Paul, in his letters, also spoke about the centrality of love in the life of a disciple, and how this is the basic message of the Old Testament Scriptures. In his letter to the church in Rome, he wrote,

> Owe no one anything, except to love each other, for the one who loves another has fulfilled the law. For the commandments, "You shall not commit adultery, You shall not murder, You shall not steal, You shall not covet," and any other commandment, are summed up in this word: "You shall love your

neighbor as yourself." Love does no wrong to a neighbor; therefore love is the fulfilling of the law.

Romans 13:8–10 ESV

Love is the fulfillment of the Law—Paul states this twice in these verses. The Greek word he used means literally to "fill up," as a bucket is filled with water or a net is filled with fish.

- How is loving others "filling up" or "completing" the Law?

Paul also characterizes Jesus's command to love others as a perpetually outstanding debt.

- Have you ever thought of the call to love others as a debt? How does this change your view of Jesus's commands in this area?

Though it may be clear that we are commanded to love God and others, it can sometimes be difficult to know how that is possible. We are inclined to think first of ourselves, so loving others well is something we struggle with. In 1 Thessalonians, Paul gives us the key to how this is possible:

May the Lord make your love increase and overflow for each other and for everyone else, just as ours does for you. May he strengthen your hearts so that you will be blameless and holy in the presence of our God and Father when our Lord Jesus comes with all his holy ones.

1 Thessalonians 3:12–13

Here we see the answer: The Lord is the one who must make our love increase and overflow for one another. We cannot manufacture Christlike love toward others. God must "strengthen [our] hearts" to love in this way.

- How does it look to rely on the Spirit to supernaturally enable us to love others?
- Have you ever shown love toward someone you didn't want to, and you could sense the Spirit working in spite of you? What was that experience like?

In 1 Thessalonians 4, Paul reiterates some of the themes we've seen: God teaches us to love others, and we should continue to pay the perpetually outstanding debt of love:

Now about your love for one another we do not need to write to you, for you yourselves have been taught by God to love each other. And in fact, you do love all of God's family throughout Macedonia. Yet we urge you, brothers and sisters, to do so more and more

1 Thessalonians 4:9–10

- What stood out to you about these verses?

Peter also wrote about loving each other, in his letter that we call 1 Peter:

Through [Christ] you believe in God, who raised him from the dead and glorified him, and so your faith and hope are in God. Now that you have purified yourselves by obeying the truth so that you have sincere love for each other, love one another deeply, from the heart. For you have been born again, not of perishable seed, but of imperishable, through the living and enduring word of God.

1 Peter 1:21–23

- What do you think it means to love each other from the heart? How would it look to love someone *not* from the heart?

We began this chapter with Jesus's words on love in the Gospel of John. Now we come full circle to John again—this time one of his letters, in which he beautifully explains what love is:

Beloved, let us love one another, for love is from God, and whoever loves has been born of God and knows God. Anyone who does not love does not know God, because God is love. In this the love of God was made manifest among us, that God sent his only Son into the world, so that we might live through him. In this is love, not that we have loved God but that he loved us and sent his Son to be the propitiation for our sins. Beloved, if God so loved us, we also ought to love one another.

1 John 4:7–11 ESV

- What stood out to you about these verses?
- How does what John wrote resonate with some of the themes we've seen so far in this chapter?

If there were any doubt about the extent of Jesus's command to love others, consider his shocking commandment in Matthew 5:

You have heard that it was said, "Love your neighbor and hate your enemy." But I tell you, love your enemies and pray for

those who persecute you, that you may be children of your
Father in heaven."

Matthew 5:43–45

Love your enemies. That is a radical commandment, but in
living that out, we are children of God. This means that we
resemble our heavenly Father by loving our enemies, because
that's exactly what Jesus did on the cross for us. We are to love
people who love us, people who don't love us, and even people
who hate us.

Key Ideas in This Study

- We are to love others as Christ loved us.
- Love is self-sacrificial.
- Love fulfills the Law.
- To love God and to love others are the two greatest
  commandments.
- Love is a perpetually outstanding debt.
- God gives us the power and strengthens our hearts to
  love others as he has loved us.
- Jesus's sacrifice defined love. He loved us first, and we
  love others as a reflection of his sacrificial love.
- Our love for others is meant to extend even to those
  who hate us.

Prayer

1. Starting with yourself, ask the group for two things:
   - A quick update on any ongoing prayer requests
   - New prayer requests

2. Write down the prayer requests as people share:

3. Ask someone in the group to close your meeting with prayer.

   - **Sample prayer:** Lord Jesus, we thank you for your love for us. We want to love you and love others as you've called us to, but we confess that we struggle in this area. We fall into the trap of thinking that people only deserve your love (or ours) if they behave in a certain way or believe what we do. We certainly withhold our love from our enemies, in direct violation of your commandment, Jesus. We are sorry for this. We need you, Holy Spirit, to strengthen our hearts and to enable us to love others as you have loved us. We trust that you will do that work in our hearts. Amen.

4

Keep Gathering

Social

A few questions to get your gathering started. This can be done during a meal or at the outset of your meeting.

- **Personal question:** Give us a quick snapshot of how things have been going since our last meeting—maybe a high and low point. (Everyone answers.)
- **Open-ended spiritual question:** What's something you feel God is teaching you right now? (A couple people share.)
- **Lead-in question to the subject of the study:** Do you feel it is important for Christians to gather with each other on a consistent basis? Why or why not?

Study

Christians have gathered together, consistently, since the beginning. Christians have gathered when conditions are perfect, and Christians have gathered (and do gather) when it is dangerous or highly inconvenient to do so. We are not called to be fair-weather gatherers; we are called to meet regularly with our brothers and sisters in Christ to encourage each other and be encouraged.

As the writer of Hebrews put it:

> Let us hold unswervingly to the hope we profess, for he who promised is faithful. And let us consider how we may spur one another on toward love and good deeds, not giving up meeting together, as some are in the habit of doing, but encouraging one another—and all the more as you see the Day approaching.
>
> Hebrews 10:23–25

- Why do you think some Christians have gotten out of the habit of meeting together consistently?
- What do you think would cause first-century Christians to neglect gathering together, and what do you think would cause modern people to forego church gatherings?
- What do you think it means to hold "unswervingly" to the hope we have in Christ, and how does gathering with other Christians help us to do that?
- How can brothers and sisters in Christ spur us on toward love and good deeds in ways that we could never do for ourselves?

When the apostle Paul wrote to his protégé Timothy about church leadership, he spoke about the Church in this way:

> Although I hope to come to you soon, I am writing you these instructions so that, if I am delayed, you will know how people ought to conduct themselves in God's household, which is the church of the living God, the pillar and foundation of the truth.
>
> 1 Timothy 3:14–15

- What are some of the ways you think people "ought to conduct themselves" as a part of the body of Christ, and why do you think that?
- Paul calls the Church "the pillar and foundation of the truth." What does this tell you about the importance of actively and consistently participating in the life of the Church?
- If someone is not gathering regularly with other Christians, how might they experience an unsteadiness in their life of faith?

In the book of Acts, we get glimpses of early churches gathering. Sometimes the circumstances were joyful; other times they were difficult or even painful. For example, after Paul and Barnabas first made their way through modern Cyprus and Turkey, planting churches along the way, they worked backward through their itinerary and gathered again with the fledgling congregations. After arriving back at their home base of Antioch, they gathered their brothers and sisters in Christ to share what God had done. We read about this in Acts 14:

> When they had preached the gospel to [Derbe] and had made many disciples, they returned to Lystra and to Iconium and to

Antioch, strengthening the souls of the disciples, encouraging them to continue in the faith, and saying that through many tribulations we must enter the kingdom of God. And when they had appointed elders for them in every church, with prayer and fasting they committed them to the Lord in whom they had believed.

Then they passed through Pisidia and came to Pamphylia. And when they had spoken the word in Perga, they went down to Attalia, and from there they sailed to Antioch, where they had been commended to the grace of God for the work that they had fulfilled. And when they arrived and gathered the church together, they declared all that God had done with them, and how he had opened a door of faith to the Gentiles. And they remained no little time with the disciples.

Acts 14:21–28 esv

- What stood out to you about this passage?
- What kind of gatherings did you see described here?
- Back up and read the first twenty verses of Acts 14. What hardships did Paul and Barnabas face, and how does this affect your view of their commitment to gathering Christians together?

In the city of Philippi in the north of Greece, Paul found a gathering of Jewish women outside the city gate. He shared the gospel with a woman named Lydia, and continued afterward to meet with her and her family:

On the Sabbath we went outside the city gate to the river, where we expected to find a place of prayer. We sat down and began to speak to the women who had gathered there. One of those listening was a woman from the city of Thyatira named Lydia, a dealer in purple cloth. She was a worshiper of God. The Lord opened her heart to respond to Paul's message. When she and the members of her household were baptized, she invited us to her home. "If you consider me a believer in the Lord," she said, "come and stay at my house." And she persuaded us.

Acts 16:13–15

- What do you notice about this event?
- The fact that the Jewish women were meeting outside of the gate implies there was no synagogue in the city—yet they were still gathering together where they could, for prayer. How does this practice challenge your commitment to gathering regularly with brothers and sisters in Christ?

Later in his evangelistic ministry, Paul visited the congregation at Troas on the west coast of modern Turkey. Paul had been there before, and while he was passing through town, he did not miss the opportunity for a meaningful gathering with the church there:

We sailed away from Philippi after the days of Unleavened Bread, and in five days we came to them at Troas, where we stayed for seven days.

On the first day of the week, when we were gathered together to break bread, Paul talked with them, intending to depart on the next day, and he prolonged his speech until midnight. There were many lamps in the upper room where we were gathered.

Acts 20:6–8 ESV

- What do you make of this scene? What does it tell you about the first-century Church?

- Can you think of a modern equivalent of this gathering?

Key Ideas in This Study

- We are called to consistently gather with other Christians.
- Gathering with the Church helps us to hold on to the hope we have in Christ.
- Gathering with the Church helps us to spur each other on to good deeds.
- The Church is the pillar and foundation of truth.
- Ideal conditions are not a necessary prerequisite for gathering with brothers and sisters in Christ.

Prayer

1. Starting with yourself, ask the group for two things:
   - A quick update on any ongoing prayer requests
   - New prayer requests

2. Write down the prayer requests as people share:

3. Ask someone in the group to close your meeting with prayer.

- **Sample prayer:** Holy Spirit, help me to prioritize gathering with the Church. I admit that I tend not to give it the priority it deserves. So often I feel that church attendance is a chore, and I do not want to feel that way. I want to feel that it is a pillar of truth in my life, and I do not want to give up gathering with the body of Christ as I have sometimes been in the habit of doing. Lead, guide, and grow me in this area. Amen.

5

Put Each Other First

Social

A few questions to get your gathering started. This can be done during a meal or at the outset of your meeting.

- **Personal question:** Give us a quick snapshot of how things have been going since our last meeting—maybe a high and low point. (Everyone answers.)
- **Open-ended spiritual question:** What's something you feel God is teaching you right now? (A couple people share.)
- **Lead-in question to the subject of the study:** What does it feel like when someone else puts your needs above their own?

Study

Selflessness is at the very heart of the Christian gospel. This is perhaps why Christians who act selfishly seem so out of step with the message and ministry of Jesus. Selfishness is not simply an irritating character trait; it is fundamentally opposed to what the Christian faith is about.

In Philippians 2, the apostle Paul quotes what many scholars consider to be an early Christian hymn about Jesus, and it speaks poetically about his selfless sacrifice:

In your relationships with one another, have the same mindset as Christ Jesus: Who, being in very nature God, did not consider equality with God something to be used to his own advantage; rather, he made himself nothing by taking the very nature of a servant, being made in human likeness. And being found in appearance as a man, he humbled himself by becoming obedient to death—even death on a cross! Therefore God exalted him to the highest place and gave him the name that is above every name, that at the name of Jesus every knee should bow, in heaven and on earth and under the earth, and every tongue acknowledge that Jesus Christ is Lord, to the glory of God the Father.

Philippians 2:5–11

- What stands out to you about these verses?
- This might be one of the earliest Christian songs ever written. When you think of these verses in that light, how do the lyrics compare with modern worship songs?
- Jesus was by nature God, but he took on the nature of a servant. What does this tell you about Jesus's love for you?

Notice the beginning of the passage above. Paul encourages Christians to look to Christ as an example. We Christians are meant to look to Jesus as the ultimate example of selflessness and seek to reflect a similar selflessness toward those around us. If, as Paul argues, Christlike selflessness is at the heart of the Christian faith, then selflessness must necessarily be at the heart of Christian community as well.

- Why is it important for Christians to seek out selflessness?
- What will happen within the Church if Christians do not put each other first?
- What might happen between Christians and non-Christians if Christians are seen to be selfish?

In Ephesians 5, Paul encouraged his readers to live a life worthy of their calling—a wise life. He wrote,

> Look carefully then how you walk, not as unwise but as wise, making the best use of the time, because the days are evil. Therefore do not be foolish, but understand what the will of the Lord is. And do not get drunk with wine, for that is debauchery, but be filled with the Spirit, addressing one another in psalms and hymns and spiritual songs, singing and making melody to the Lord with your heart, giving thanks always and for everything to God the Father in the name of our Lord Jesus Christ, submitting to one another out of reverence for Christ.
>
> Ephesians 5:15–21 ESV

- How do these verses relate to the idea of selflessness within the Church?

- If we are filled with the Spirit, Paul writes, we will do a number of things: encourage each other, sing, give thanks—and also *submit* to each other.* What does this tell you about how we go about submitting to one another? Can we do this in our own strength?
- How is the end of this passage similar to what we read in Philippians 2?

In his first letter to the Thessalonian church, Paul urged the congregation to live in a distinctly Christlike way. The Thessalonians were new believers living in a city that was sometimes antagonistic to them. Paul wrote to them:

> We urge you, brothers and sisters, warn those who are idle and disruptive, encourage the disheartened, help the weak, be patient with everyone. Make sure that nobody pays back wrong for wrong, but always strive to do what is good for each other and for everyone else. Rejoice always, pray continually, give thanks in all circumstances; for this is God's will for you in Christ Jesus.
>
> 1 Thessalonians 5:14–18

- What strikes you about these verses?
- Where in this passage do you see Paul encouraging selflessness?
- How do rejoicing, praying, and giving thanks help us to put others first?

In Ephesians 5, Paul suggested that mutual submission flowed out of being filled with the Holy Spirit—meaning that we cannot manufacture a selfless attitude or genuinely put others first

---

*The Greek word for *submit* is ὑποτάσσω (*hypotassō*), which means to place or rank something below something else.

in our own strength. Paul elaborates on this important idea in Galatians 5:

> You, my brothers and sisters, were called to be free. But do not use your freedom to indulge the flesh; rather, serve one another humbly in love. For the entire law is fulfilled in keeping this one command: "Love your neighbor as yourself." If you bite and devour each other, watch out or you will be destroyed by each other. So I say, walk by the Spirit, and you will not gratify the desires of the flesh. For the flesh desires what is contrary to the Spirit, and the Spirit what is contrary to the flesh.
>
> Galatians 5:13–17

- Have you ever seen someone serve someone else humbly, in love—as Paul describes here? What was it like to witness, and how did it affect you?
- Jesus called us to love our neighbors as ourselves, which Paul echoes here. How is putting someone else first loving them as you love yourself?
- Paul explains that by walking in the Spirit we will not gratify our fleshly desire to put ourselves first. Have you asked the Holy Spirit to give you a selfless, servant's heart? Why or why not?

When Jesus was about to be betrayed by Judas and walk through the final events of his earthly life, he set a clear and public example of how we are to put each other first:

> [Jesus] rose from supper. He laid aside his outer garments, and taking a towel, tied it around his waist. Then he poured water into a basin and began to wash the disciples' feet and to wipe them with the towel that was wrapped around him. He came to Simon Peter, who said to him, "Lord, do you wash my

feet?" Jesus answered him, "What I am doing you do not understand now, but afterward you will understand." Peter said to him, "You shall never wash my feet." Jesus answered him, "If I do not wash you, you have no share with me." Simon Peter said to him, "Lord, not my feet only but also my hands and my head!" Jesus said to him, "The one who has bathed does not need to wash, except for his feet, but is completely clean. And you are clean, but not every one of you." For he knew who was to betray him; that was why he said, "Not all of you are clean."

When he had washed their feet and put on his outer garments and resumed his place, he said to them, "Do you understand what I have done to you? You call me Teacher and Lord, and you are right, for so I am. If I then, your Lord and Teacher, have washed your feet, you also ought to wash one another's feet. For I have given you an example, that you also should do just as I have done to you."

John 13:4–15 ESV

- What stands out to you about these verses?
- The disciples' feet—like most people's feet of that era—would have been dirty. They spent their waking hours outside and walked almost everywhere. To wash someone's feet was to literally get your hands dirty and give them the gift of feeling clean. In what ways can you serve others like this?
- Jesus specifically said this was an example for us to follow. Why do you think we have such a hard time obeying him and putting others first?

In perhaps the clearest command to put others first, Jesus said:

Anyone who wants to be first must be the very last, and the servant of all.

Mark 9:35

Key Ideas in This Study

- Selflessness is at the heart of the Christian gospel.
- If Christlike selflessness is at the heart of the Christian faith, then selflessness must necessarily be at the heart of Christian community.
- Christ is our example of what true selflessness looks like.
- Submission to one another is accomplished by the Holy Spirit.
- Serving others humbly is an example of loving our neighbors as ourselves.
- Because Jesus washed his disciples' feet, we should have the same heart posture toward others.

Prayer

1. Starting with yourself, ask the group for two things:
   - A quick update on any ongoing prayer requests
   - New prayer requests

2. Write down the prayer requests as people share:

3. Ask someone in the group to close your meeting with prayer.

- **Sample prayer:** Lord Jesus, I want to follow your example of washing feet. I want to follow your example of taking on the nature of a servant. I want selflessness to take root and grow in my life, and I want selfishness to wither. Holy Spirit, I know you must do this work in me for it to be true; I pray that you will and that my heart will be willing. Amen.

6

Build Each Other Up

Social

A few questions to get your gathering started. This can be done during a meal or at the outset of your meeting.

- **Personal question:** Give us a quick snapshot of how things have been going since our last meeting—maybe a high and low point. (Everyone answers.)
- **Open-ended spiritual question:** What's something you feel God is teaching you right now? (A couple people share.)
- **Lead-in question to the subject of the study:** What do you think is the difference between putting someone else first and building that person up?

Study

Last chapter, we explored the biblical mandate that we are supposed to put each other first. The way to be first, according to Jesus, is to be last—a very countercultural notion in the ancient world and in our time. We are to look to Jesus as our perfect example of sacrificial selflessness.

Most people would agree that selflessness is a good idea. Jesus and the other New Testament writers spoke often of putting others first. But we can imagine a scenario in our lives when we might put someone's interests ahead of our own and hold a grudge against them for it. We might do the right thing but be embittered because we do not think we should have to put someone ahead of ourselves. Or perhaps we feel we are putting someone first too often or they are not returning the favor. There are many opportunities for frustration, even if we are seeking to do the right thing and put others first.

- Have you ever felt frustration in this area before? How did you handle it?
- What is the place of our motives in putting others first?

In this chapter, we will explore an idea that will build upon last chapter's material and help prevent us from becoming frustrated when we put others first. It will guard us from becoming begrudging servants. That concept is building other people up.

Putting other people first is often an exercise in getting out of the way or not doing something we would like to do. We allow others the right of way. We allow others to get the attention or credit. We allow other people's ideas to be implemented. We do not assert ourselves. But to build someone up is a more deliberate endeavor. To build someone up means not only allowing them to be first, but proactively finding ways to help them flourish.

- Who in your life has built you up?
- Whom have you built up, and what was your experience in doing so?
- Is it possible to build someone up without putting them first?

In some of Paul's letters, he dealt with a very sensitive subject that to our modern minds seems mundane. To first-century Christians, however, it was highly divisive and controversial. The subject was food: what Christians could eat and when they should or shouldn't eat it. Christians of a Jewish background were sensitive about certain foods because of the purity laws they were accustomed to. Christians of a Greco-Roman background did not grow up with the same food restrictions. Also, there was the matter of whether any Christian—regardless of background—should eat food that was sold in the marketplace after having been sacrificed to a pagan deity. Some felt it was wrong or blasphemous to do so. Others felt it wasn't a problem because the pagan deities weren't real. All that to say, eating together was often divisive—or at least awkward—in many first-century Christian communities. People were poised to take offense with each other.

- Does this situation sound similar to any sensitive cultural matters facing the Church today?

In his letter to the Galatian Christians, Paul describes a confrontation he had over this issue with Peter. When Peter first visited the city where Paul lived (Antioch), he ate certain foods with gentile Christians, but when a delegation of Jewish Christians came from Jerusalem, Peter stopped sharing a table with the gentile Christians in order to not offend the Jewish Christians who were visiting. Look what Paul wrote about his argument with Peter (whom he calls by his Aramaic name, Cephas):

> When Cephas came to Antioch, I opposed him to his face, because he stood condemned. For before certain men came from James, he was eating with the Gentiles; but when they came he drew back and separated himself, fearing the circumcision party. And the rest of the Jews acted hypocritically along with him, so that even Barnabas was led astray by their hypocrisy. But when I saw that their conduct was not in step with the truth of the gospel, I said to Cephas before them all, "If you, though a Jew, live like a Gentile and not like a Jew, how can you force the Gentiles to live like Jews?"
>
> Galatians 2:11–14 ESV

- What do you make of Paul's response to Peter's actions?
- How does this passage illuminate the subject of putting others first and building each other up?

In Galatians 2, Paul described an event that had to do with this divisive food issue. In Romans 14, Paul teaches about that same subject. He writes,

> The one who eats everything must not treat with contempt the one who does not, and the one who does not eat everything must not judge the one who does, for God has accepted them. Who are you to judge someone else's servant? . . . Therefore let us stop passing judgment on one another. Instead, make up

your mind not to put any stumbling block or obstacle in the way of a brother or sister.

Romans 14:3–4, 13

- What do you notice about these verses?
- How are Christians supposed to treat each other when they disagree over a sensitive issue like this?
- How does this passage speak to the matter of putting others first?

When we continue reading that same passage in Romans 14, we see that Paul does not stop at putting others first. He does not merely suggest avoiding bothering someone else when it comes to food. He takes it another step and encourages the Roman Christians to actively build each other up:

Let us therefore make every effort to do what leads to peace and to mutual edification.

Romans 14:19

- What stands out to you about this rich verse?
- The words *mutual edification* are an English translation of Paul's words in ancient Greek, which are more literally translated as *building up one another*. Paul is telling us to make every effort to pursue peace and build each other up. How can you apply this command in your personal life?
- How might the Church apply this command to foster growth and health?

In the next chapter, Paul gives an example of how the Romans might go about building each other up:

> May the God of hope fill you with all joy and peace as you trust in him, so that you may overflow with hope by the power of the Holy Spirit. I myself am convinced, my brothers and sisters, that you yourselves are full of goodness, filled with knowledge and competent to instruct one another. Yet I have written you quite boldly on some points to remind you of them again, because of the grace God gave me to be a minister of Christ Jesus to the Gentiles. He gave me the priestly duty of proclaiming the gospel of God, so that the Gentiles might become an offering acceptable to God, sanctified by the Holy Spirit.
>
> Romans 15:13–16

- What do you make of Paul's statement that the Roman Christians are "filled with knowledge and competent to instruct one another"? How might Christians today build each other up in this way?
- Paul prays that the Romans would overflow with the power of the Holy Spirit and speaks of his own ministry as being an outgrowth of God's grace. What does this tell you about how we should think about our own growth and building each other up?

In 1 Thessalonians, Paul encouraged the relatively new believers in Thessalonica to love and build each other up and continue to do so more and more. Consider these three short passages:

> As for other matters, brothers and sisters, we instructed you how to live in order to please God, as in fact you are living.

Now we ask you and urge you in the Lord Jesus to do this more and more.

1 Thessalonians 4:1

About your love for one another we do not need to write to you, for you yourselves have been taught by God to love each other. And in fact, you do love all of God's family throughout Macedonia. Yet we urge you, brothers and sisters, to do so more and more.

1 Thessalonians 4:9–10

Encourage one another and build each other up, just as in fact you are doing.

1 Thessalonians 5:11

- What stands out to you about these verses, and how are they relevant to your personal walk with the Lord?
- How do they matter for the Church today?

In Corinth, the church was experiencing disunity and confusion over the gifts of the Holy Spirit and what should happen during worship gatherings. Into this fraught moment, Paul wrote,

What then shall we say, brothers and sisters? When you come together, each of you has a hymn, or a word of instruction, a revelation, a tongue or an interpretation. Everything must be done so that the church may be built up.

1 Corinthians 14:26

- Without naming names or being unnecessarily critical, what are some practices you see in churches today that are common but do not build up the church? What practices are missing?

- How can you help?

Key Ideas in This Study

- Building each other up is the next step beyond putting others first.
- When dealing with a culturally divisive issue like the first-century Christians did regarding food, we are called to seek opportunities to put others first and build them up.
- Christians, filled with knowledge and the Holy Spirit, are competent to instruct one another on matters of faith.
- God's grace and the Holy Spirit enable us to live out the call to put others first and build each other up.
- Worship gatherings should be about building up the Church.

Prayer

1. Starting with yourself, ask the group for two things:
   - A quick update on any ongoing prayer requests
   - New prayer requests

2. Write down the prayer requests as people share:

3. Ask someone in the group to close your meeting with prayer.

   • **Sample prayer:** Lord Jesus, I want to be a person who puts others first. But I do not want to stop there. I want to build others up. I want to be someone that others would describe as encouraging and humble. Help me, Holy Spirit, to grow into this kind of person. Mold me into your image, Jesus, so that I might glorify you and encourage others. Amen.

7

Clothed in Christlikeness

Social

A few questions to get your gathering started. This can be done during a meal or at the outset of your meeting.

- **Personal question:** Give us a quick snapshot of how things have been going since our last meeting—maybe a high and low point. (Everyone answers.)
- **Open-ended spiritual question:** What's something you feel God is teaching you right now? (A couple people share.)
- **Lead-in question to the subject of the study:** What do you think are the characteristics of Christlikeness?

Study

It's no secret that Christians are prone to conflict and that the Church has had to cope with various types of internal divisions over the last twenty centuries. Today, we can think of many aspects of modern life that cause grumbling and struggles within the Church: theological quarreling, differences in political ideology, disagreements about how church ministries should be structured, etc.

- What are some public disagreements happening within the Church right now? In what ways do you think they're being handled well or mishandled?
- What conflicts have you witnessed or been a part of in your own church, and what impression did the experience leave on you?

It is remarkable how the first-century Church held together in spite of the deep, painful, socially reinforced boundaries between people. The Roman world was brutally hierarchical, with those on the upper end of society exploiting and dehumanizing those who were on the lower end of the social spectrum. Men ruled over women. Masters ruled over slaves. The rich ruled over the poor. The Romans ruled over the other peoples of the Mediterranean world.

The Holy Spirit, of course, is the one who made the surprising unity of the Church possible. I believe the way he did it was to help the Christians see that breaking social barriers wasn't about trying to be a nice person or striving after a certain piety or morality. It was about embracing a completely new identity given to us by Christ. Jesus spoke of being born again. Paul spoke of Christians as new creations in Christ. The only way we can have unity in the Church is by believing and living out this amazing reality.

In Colossians 3, Paul wrote about our new identity and its practical expressions. Let's read a longer passage once in its entirety and then look closely at shorter portions of it to make sure we don't miss anything. First, read it once through:

> Since, then, you have been raised with Christ, set your hearts on things above, where Christ is, seated at the right hand of God. Set your minds on things above, not on earthly things. For you died, and your life is now hidden with Christ in God. When Christ, who is your life, appears, then you also will appear with him in glory.
>
> . . . Do not lie to each other, since you have taken off your old self with its practices and have put on the new self, which is being renewed in knowledge in the image of its Creator. Here there is no Gentile or Jew, circumcised or uncircumcised, barbarian, Scythian, slave or free, but Christ is all, and is in all.
>
> Therefore, as God's chosen people, holy and dearly loved, clothe yourselves with compassion, kindness, humility, gentleness and patience. Bear with each other and forgive one another if any of you has a grievance against someone. Forgive as the Lord forgave you. And over all these virtues put on love, which binds them all together in perfect unity.
>
> Let the peace of Christ rule in your hearts, since as members of one body you were called to peace. And be thankful. Let the message of Christ dwell among you richly as you teach and admonish one another with all wisdom through psalms, hymns, and songs from the Spirit, singing to God with gratitude in your hearts. And whatever you do, whether in word or deed, do it all in the name of the Lord Jesus, giving thanks to God the Father through him.
>
> Colossians 3:1–4, 9–17

- What stood out to you about this passage?
- Anything surprising or challenging?

Let's look back now on the first four verses:

Since, then, you have been raised with Christ, set your hearts on things above, where Christ is, seated at the right hand of God. Set your minds on things above, not on earthly things. For you died, and your life is now hidden with Christ in God. When Christ, who is your life, appears, then you also will appear with him in glory.

- What do you think it means to set your heart on things above? How does this look on a daily basis?
- What do you make of the phrase "your life is now hidden with Christ in God"? How does this affect your view of yourself and your life?

Paul continues his discussion of this new identity:

Do not lie to each other, since you have taken off your old self with its practices and have put on the new self, which is being renewed in knowledge in the image of its Creator. Here there is no Gentile or Jew, circumcised or uncircumcised, barbarian, Scythian, slave or free, but Christ is all, and is in all.

- What do you think about this concept of an old or new self? When you became a Christian, what surprised you about your new self? In what ways do you see vestiges of your old self in your life today?
- Paul breaks down the social, religious, and ethnic boundaries that threatened to divide the Church—saying that Christ is all and is in all. What do you think that means: Christ is all and is in all?

Next, Paul begins to explain in detail how it looks to live out our new identities in Christ.

Therefore, as God's chosen people, holy and dearly loved, clothe yourselves with compassion, kindness, humility, gentleness and patience. Bear with each other and forgive one another if any of you has a grievance against someone. Forgive as the Lord forgave you. And over all these virtues put on love, which binds them all together in perfect unity.

Let the peace of Christ rule in your hearts, since as members of one body you were called to peace. And be thankful. Let the message of Christ dwell among you richly as you teach and admonish one another with all wisdom through psalms, hymns, and songs from the Spirit, singing to God with gratitude in your hearts. And whatever you do, whether in word or deed, do it all in the name of the Lord Jesus, giving thanks to God the Father through him.

- What do you think it means to "clothe yourself" with compassion, kindness, humility, gentleness, and patience? How is this different from trying to be compassionate, kind, humble, gentle, patient, etc.?
- What qualities of Christlikeness stand out to you in the second paragraph above? Which do you personally struggle with, and why do you think that is?
- Paul says that whatever we do should be done in the name of the Lord Jesus. What do you think that means, and how can you apply this in your life?

Maintaining unity in the Church, avoiding conflict, and honoring the Lord are the result of the Holy Spirit's work in our lives as we embrace our new identities in Christ. It is not about striving to be moral or working hard to be publicly pious. Our lives are hidden in Christ. We have been born again. We are new creations in Christ. We must clothe ourselves with Christ, as Paul put it. He says it this way in Galatians 3:

In Christ Jesus you are all children of God through faith, for all of you who were baptized into Christ have clothed yourselves with Christ. There is neither Jew nor Gentile, neither slave nor free, nor is there male and female, for you are all one in Christ Jesus. If you belong to Christ, then you are Abraham's seed, and heirs according to the promise.

Galatians 3:26–29

- What do you think about this text? How does it relate to what we just read in Colossians?

In one of Peter's letters, he also picked up on this idea of clothing ourselves in Christlikeness:

All of you, clothe yourselves with humility toward one another, because, "God opposes the proud but shows favor to the humble." Humble yourselves, therefore, under God's mighty hand, that he may lift you up in due time.

1 Peter 5:5–6

- What do you think about Peter's words? How does this connect to what Paul said on the matter?

Key Ideas in This Study

- The Holy Spirit makes unity and Christlikeness possible.
- Christlikeness isn't about striving for morality or public piety; it's about embracing a new identity in Christ.
- We are called to be clothed in Christlikeness.

Prayer

1. Starting with yourself, ask the group for two things:
   - A quick update on any ongoing prayer requests
   - New prayer requests

2. Write down the prayer requests as people share:

3. Ask someone in the group to close your meeting with prayer.

   - **Sample prayer:** Holy Spirit, I want to maintain unity with my brothers and sisters in Christ, and the way to do that is to rely on you to cultivate Christlikeness in me and in spite of me. I don't want to just try to be nice or moral or godly; I want to be clothed in Christlikeness. I confess I don't know exactly what that looks like, but I trust that you do and that you can bring it about. Please do that work in my heart. Amen.

8

Humble and Hospitable

Social

A few questions to get your gathering started. This can be done during a meal or at the outset of your meeting.

- **Personal question:** Give us a quick snapshot of how things have been going since our last meeting—maybe a high and low point. (Everyone answers.)
- **Open-ended spiritual question:** What's something you feel God is teaching you right now? (A couple people share.)
- **Lead-in question to the subject of the study:** What is the relationship between humility and hospitality?

Study

Hospitality is a hallmark of humility, because hospitality is a form of sharing. We are sharing our lives, our homes, our time with other people. In order to be willing to genuinely share in that way—especially consistently—we have to be focused on others.

- Who is the most hospitable person or family you've ever known? What were they like as people?
- Have you ever known someone who is arrogant or unkind and also genuinely hospitable? Why do you think hospitality and arrogance don't go together?

Humility and hospitality are external evidence of the Lord's internal work in our hearts. They are signs that Christ has transformed us. Consider Paul's words in Ephesians 4:

> As a prisoner for the Lord, then, I urge you to live a life worthy of the calling you have received. Be completely humble and gentle; be patient, bearing with one another in love. Make every effort to keep the unity of the Spirit through the bond of peace. There is one body and one Spirit, just as you were called to one hope when you were called; one Lord, one faith, one baptism; one God and Father of all, who is over all and through all and in all.
>
> Ephesians 4:1–6

- Paul urges us to live lives worthy of our calling. What are the first qualities he describes as a follow-up to that statement?
- How is hospitality related to maintaining unity in the Church? How is hospitality a form of "bearing with one another in love"?

In another of Paul's letters, he explicitly tells us to be hospitable:

Share with the Lord's people who are in need. Practice hospitality.

Romans 12:13

- Paul commands hospitality right after encouraging us to share with those in need. How is hospitality taking care of those in need? What needs are met in hospitality?
- How is humility related to generosity?

In one of Peter's letters, he speaks of hospitality:

Above all, love each other deeply, because love covers over a multitude of sins. Offer hospitality to one another without grumbling.

1 Peter 4:8–9

- Peter begins by discussing love between brothers and sisters in Christ. He follows this by encouraging us to offer hospitality to each other. How are love and hospitality related?
- In what ways does grumbling undermine hospitality?
- How is being inhospitable out of step with the gospel?

In another apostle's letter, we again encounter this notion of hospitality. Third John is a short, personal letter from John to a brother in Christ named Gaius, and the subject matter has to do with taking care of others:

The elder, to my dear friend Gaius, whom I love in the truth. Dear friend, I pray that you may enjoy good health and that all may go well with you, even as your soul is getting along well. It gave me great joy when some believers came and testified about your faithfulness to the truth, telling how you continue to walk in it. I have no greater joy than to hear that my children are walking in the truth.

Dear friend, you are faithful in what you are doing for the brothers and sisters, even though they are strangers to you. They have told the church about your love. Please send them on their way in a manner that honors God. It was for the sake of the Name that they went out, receiving no help from the pagans. We ought therefore to show hospitality to such people so that we may work together for the truth.

3 John 1:1–8

- What do you notice about these verses?
- How would you describe John and Gaius's relationship based on these few verses?
- What word does John use to describe Gaius's actions?
- What is one reason for showing hospitality, according to the final sentence of this passage?

We have seen that hospitality is woven together with character traits such as humility, love, and faithfulness. But why would Paul, Peter, John, and others speak so often of hospitality? The answer is that it goes back to Jesus's character and teaching.

Jesus's famous parable of the good Samaritan is about countercultural hospitality. Here's what happened leading up to Jesus's telling of the parable:

A lawyer stood up to put him to the test, saying, "Teacher, what shall I do to inherit eternal life?" He said to him, "What is written in the Law? How do you read it?" And he answered, "You shall love the Lord your God with all your heart and with all your soul and with all your strength and with all your mind, and your neighbor as yourself." And he said to him, "You have answered correctly; do this, and you will live."

But he, desiring to justify himself, said to Jesus, "And who is my neighbor?"

Luke 10:25–29 ESV

- What do you notice about this exchange between Jesus and the expert in the Law?

Next comes the parable itself:

Jesus replied, "A man was going down from Jerusalem to Jericho, and he fell among robbers, who stripped him and beat him and departed, leaving him half dead. Now by chance a priest was going down that road, and when he saw him he passed by on the other side. So likewise a Levite, when he came to the place and saw him, passed by on the other side. But a Samaritan, as he journeyed, came to where he was, and when he saw him, he had compassion. He went to him and bound up his wounds, pouring on oil and wine. Then he set him on his own animal and brought him to an inn and took care of him. And the next day he took out two denarii and gave them to the innkeeper, saying, 'Take care of him, and whatever more you spend, I will repay you when I come back."

Luke 10:30–35 ESV

- What do you notice about this parable?
- What words would you use to describe the Samaritan's behavior?

The parable of the good Samaritan and the subject of hospitality are about loving our neighbor as ourselves. This is proven by the follow-up question Jesus asked after telling the parable:

> "Which of these three, do you think, proved to be a neighbor to the man who fell among the robbers?" He said, "The one who showed him mercy." And Jesus said to him, "You go, and do likewise."
>
> Luke 10:36–37 ESV

- How is hospitality related to mercy?
- Jesus said, "Go and do likewise." How can we show this sort of hospitality in our lives today?

Key Ideas in This Study

- Humility and hospitality go together.
- We are called to be generously hospitable, even to strangers.
- Hospitality is loving our neighbors as ourselves.
- Hospitality is a form of faithfulness.

Prayer

1. Starting with yourself, ask the group for two things:
   - A quick update on any ongoing prayer requests
   - New prayer requests

2. Write down the prayer requests as people share:

3. Ask someone in the group to close your meeting with prayer.

- **Sample prayer:** Lord Jesus, help me to be hospitable to others not because I'm just trying to be a nice person or follow your rules, but because I understand on a deep level that you accepted me in spite of my many sins. I did not deserve your love, forgiveness, and acceptance, but you invited me to be close to you—to be a member of your family. You welcomed me in, and as a reflection of that, help me to welcome others. Amen.

9

Dodging Divisions

Social

A few questions to get your gathering started. This can be done during a meal or at the outset of your meeting.

- **Personal question:** Give us a quick snapshot of how things have been going since our last meeting—maybe a high and low point. (Everyone answers.)
- **Open-ended spiritual question:** What's something you feel God is teaching you right now? (A couple people share.)
- **Lead-in question to the subject of the study:** What's the most foolish argument you've ever gotten into? What was the outcome, and how would you handle it differently if you could do it over again?

Study

Christians have always argued, both with each other and with others outside of the Church. Interpersonal conflicts, disagreements about how to conduct worship services, arguments about church priorities—these have been around since the Church was born.

Some people enjoy arguing, and our age of social media has provided fertile soil for people like that. Many people, by contrast, do not enjoy arguing. Whether or not we seek out conflict, we live in a time in which there is an endless parade of possible arguments marching past us every single day. We must be wise about which fights are worth picking, and we must admit that most arguments accomplish very little. Consider this proverb:

> An unfriendly person pursues selfish ends and against all sound judgment starts quarrels. Fools find no pleasure in understanding but delight in airing their own opinions.
>
> Proverbs 18:1–2

- What do you notice about these verses?
- Starting quarrels is "against all sound judgment." Why do you think that is?
- A quarrelsome person is "unfriendly," according to this proverb. How is it unfriendly to be a person who argues frequently?
- This proverb also links the idea of starting quarrels with pursuing selfish ends. In what ways is it selfish to regularly pursue conflicts?
- The writer suggests the motives of a quarrelsome person are in the wrong place: speaking one's mind instead

of seeking understanding. Why do you think it's easier to voice our opinions than to listen to others?

When it comes to leadership within the Church, the New Testament writers suggest that consistently engaging in conflict is out of step with Christlikeness. Of course, there are certain matters that demand confrontation (e.g., distortions of the gospel, disunity in the Church, all varieties of abusive behavior, etc.), but we should not be argumentative people or relish conflict. In his letters to Timothy and Titus, the apostle Paul gives these leaders insight and instructions regarding conflict. He wants them to set a Christlike example, and part of that is treating conflict seriously but graciously. In 2 Timothy, Paul wrote:

> Flee the evil desires of youth and pursue righteousness, faith, love and peace, along with those who call on the Lord out of a pure heart. Don't have anything to do with foolish and stupid arguments, because you know they produce quarrels. And the Lord's servant must not be quarrelsome but must be kind to everyone, able to teach, not resentful. Opponents must be gently instructed, in the hope that God will grant them repentance leading them to a knowledge of the truth, and that they will come to their senses and escape from the trap of the devil, who has taken them captive to do his will.
>
> 2 Timothy 2:22–26

- Paul lays out what followers of Christ should be pursuing: righteousness, faith, love, and peace. How are these qualities out of sync with an argumentative spirit?
- Next, Paul instructs Timothy not to have "anything to do with foolish and stupid arguments." How might this

look in your life? How can you lovingly refuse to be involved with foolish arguments?

- Then Paul gives the reason for this: The Lord's servant must not be quarrelsome, but kind to everyone. How does being quarrelsome undermine our efforts to be kind?

- When we encounter someone who is looking to argue with us, how are we to respond to them, according to this passage?

- What should we be willing to argue about? What sorts of conflict are biblical—even Christlike?

In Paul's letter to Titus, he articulates the gospel in a beautiful way, describing our life before Christ:

> We ourselves were once foolish, disobedient, led astray, slaves to various passions and pleasures, passing our days in malice and envy, hated by others and hating one another. But when the goodness and loving kindness of God our Savior appeared, he saved us, not because of works done by us in righteousness, but according to his own mercy, by the washing of regeneration and renewal of the Holy Spirit, whom he poured out on us richly through Jesus Christ our Savior, so that being justified by his grace we might become heirs according to the hope of eternal life.
>
> Titus 3:3–7 ESV

- What did you notice about these verses?
- What stands out to you about how Paul characterized our life before Jesus?

In the next few verses, Paul insists that Titus and those he leads live out their new identities in Christ. He wants them to live life in light of what Jesus did for them:

> This is a trustworthy saying. And I want you to stress these things, so that those who have trusted in God may be careful to devote themselves to doing what is good. These things are excellent and profitable for everyone. But avoid foolish controversies and genealogies and arguments and quarrels about the law, because these are unprofitable and useless. Warn a divisive person once, and then warn them a second time. After that, have nothing to do with them.
>
> Titus 3:8–10

- Paul instructs Titus—as he did Timothy—to avoid foolish controversies. In this case he gives specific examples: arguments over heritage and interpretation of the Old Testament Law. Paul says they are "unprofitable and useless." What arguments today, within the Church, do you feel are "unprofitable and useless"?

- Give one example of an argument you started that—in retrospect—was "unprofitable and useless."

- Paul calls these arguments "foolish," which is a characteristic of our lives without Christ. In what ways does unnecessary arguing reflect our lives without Jesus?

- Paul says to "have nothing to do with them" after a divisive person is warned twice to change their ways. Paul does not mean for the Christian community to shun them, but rather to cease engaging with them on the matters they are using to cause division. What's the best way to go about this?

In 1 Timothy, Paul speaks about divisions and conflict within the Church, touching on some of the same themes we saw in the passages above. He is speaking to Timothy about potential leaders in the Church:

> Now the overseer is to be above reproach, faithful to his wife, temperate, self-controlled, respectable, hospitable, able to teach, not given to drunkenness, not violent but gentle, not quarrelsome, not a lover of money.
>
> 1 Timothy 3:2–3

> If anyone teaches otherwise and does not agree to the sound instruction of our Lord Jesus Christ and to godly teaching, they are conceited and understand nothing. They have an unhealthy interest in controversies and quarrels about words that result in envy, strife, malicious talk, evil suspicions and constant friction between people of corrupt mind, who have been robbed of the truth and who think that godliness is a means to financial gain. But godliness with contentment is great gain.
>
> 1 Timothy 6:3–6

- What do you notice about Paul's words in 1 Timothy?
- Paul says that Church leaders should not be quarrelsome. What qualities does he list that are out of step with a quarrelsome nature?
- Paul suggests that those who teach something other than the true gospel of Jesus Christ are conceited and will exhibit an unhealthy interest in controversies. Have you observed this in the Church today? What do you think is the connection between unbiblical teaching and being quarrelsome?

When Paul was writing to Timothy and Titus about the corrosive effects of arguments within the Church, he wasn't speaking in theory; he experienced painful conflict, especially with the church in Corinth.

Apparently, some of the Christians in Corinth were fighting over leadership. Some were fans of Paul, others were more interested in following another leader, Apollos.* Paul had no time for this foolish controversy, so he confronted and dismantled the flawed thinking of the Corinthians:

> I, brothers, could not address you as spiritual people, but as people of the flesh, as infants in Christ. I fed you with milk, not solid food, for you were not ready for it. And even now you are not yet ready, for you are still of the flesh. For while there is jealousy and strife among you, are you not of the flesh and behaving only in a human way? For when one says, "I follow Paul," and another, "I follow Apollos," are you not being merely human?
>
> What then is Apollos? What is Paul? Servants through whom you believed, as the Lord assigned to each. I planted, Apollos watered, but God gave the growth. So neither he who plants nor he who waters is anything, but only God who gives the growth. He who plants and he who waters are one, and each will receive his wages according to his labor. For we are God's fellow workers. You are God's field, God's building.
>
> 1 Corinthians 3:1–9 ESV

- At the beginning of this text, Paul is describing the quarrelsome attitudes of the Corinthians as a marker of immaturity. What stood out to you about how Paul described them?

*See Acts 18:24–28.

- Have you ever thought of being argumentative as a mark of spiritual immaturity?
- What is Paul's response to this conflict? How does he dismantle the comparison game that the Corinthians were playing?
- Who, according to Paul, gets all the credit for growth among the Corinthians?
- What term does Paul use to describe his relationship with Apollos and other leaders?

A little later in 1 Corinthians, Paul addresses another controversy that is causing divisions. In this case, it has to do with worship services. There are arguments and fractures over the observance of the Lord's Supper. It seems that the wealthier members of the congregation are eating and drinking their fill, while the poorer members of the congregation have little or nothing to eat or drink. The Corinthians are not sharing well, and are preserving social divisions rather than breaking them down:

> In the following instructions I do not commend you, because when you come together it is not for the better but for the worse. For, in the first place, when you come together as a church, I hear that there are divisions among you. And I believe it in part, for there must be factions among you in order that those who are genuine among you may be recognized. When you come together, it is not the Lord's supper that you eat. For in eating, each one goes ahead with his own meal. One goes hungry, another gets drunk. What! Do you not have houses to eat and drink in? Or do you despise the church of God

and humiliate those who have nothing? What shall I say to you? Shall I commend you in this? No, I will not.

1 Corinthians 11:17–22 ESV

- What did you notice about these verses?
- How is this a foolish controversy?
- What were the Corinthians missing about the nature of the Church that caused them to create this situation?
- What modern situations do you feel resemble this one?

Key Ideas in This Study

- To be quarrelsome is to be unfriendly, selfish, immature, and unwise.
- We should avoid foolish and stupid controversies.
- Foolishness was a characteristic of our identities without Christ.
- Engaging in unnecessary quarrels is unwise and out of step with growing in Christlikeness.
- The comparison game leads to foolish arguments.
- A lack of commitment to the truth breeds an unhealthy interest in controversy.

Prayer

1. Starting with yourself, ask the group for two things:
   - A quick update on any ongoing prayer requests
   - New prayer requests

2. Write down the prayer requests as people share:

3. Ask someone in the group to close your meeting with prayer.

   - **Sample prayer:** Heavenly Father, I recognize that I have the capability of being an argumentative person. I am sorry for the foolish controversies I have started or indulged. I do not want to be divisive, unwise, selfish, and immature. I desire to be a wise, selfless, mature unifier. For that to be true of me, I need you—Holy Spirit—to cultivate those qualities in me. Please mold me into your image, Jesus. I trust you to do that. Amen.

10

Givers of Courage

Social

A few questions to get your gathering started. This can be done during a meal or at the outset of your meeting.

- **Personal question:** Give us a quick snapshot of how things have been going since our last meeting—maybe a high and low point. (Everyone answers.)
- **Open-ended spiritual question:** What's something you feel God is teaching you right now? (A couple people share.)
- **Lead-in question to the subject of the study:** What do you think it means to encourage one another in our journeys of faith?

Study

Each follower of Jesus struggles at various times and in various ways. Sometimes we have doubts about God or his plan for our lives. At other times, especially when we face some form of suffering, we might wonder about God or feel disillusioned or disappointed with the Church. Sometimes we struggle with a particular sin that makes us feel distant from God. At other times, the cares of life just overwhelm us, and we find that we've de-prioritized our spiritual lives.

We are called to encourage each other in our lives of faith. But what does that mean? We long to be encouraged, but sometimes we're not sure what would actually encourage us. We would like to be encouragers of others, but sometimes it's hard to know what to say or do—especially when we have our own struggles.

The etymology of the English word *encourage* gives us part of the answer: en-courage. It means to infuse courage into someone's life or a situation. To be an encourager means to be a giver of courage. That's part of what it means to encourage—to give courage. The Greek word in the New Testament that we translate into the English word *encourage* is παρακαλέω (*parakaleō*). This word tells us *how* we can be givers of courage. *Parakaleō* means to call to one's side. It's the image of bringing someone close to you and comforting them, like a parent putting their arm around one of their children and speaking reassuring words to them.

Encouraging, therefore, is giving courage to someone by coming alongside them and speaking truth and life into their situation.

- What do you think about this understanding of what it means to encourage?
- Who has encouraged you in your faith in this way?

When we look at the New Testament, we see a number of examples of what it looks like to be an encourager. We will look at three instances in Paul's letters. One has to do with encouraging each other to embrace our identities in Christ. Another has to do with bearing each other's burdens. The third example is about reminding each other of the truth.

In 1 Thessalonians 5, Paul wrote to the church in Thessalonica to encourage them in the face of persecution and many struggles:

> But you are not in darkness, brothers, for that day to surprise you like a thief. For you are all children of light, children of the day. We are not of the night or of the darkness. So then let us not sleep, as others do, but let us keep awake and be sober. For those who sleep, sleep at night, and those who get drunk, are drunk at night. But since we belong to the day, let us be sober, having put on the breastplate of faith and love, and for a helmet the hope of salvation. For God has not destined us for wrath, but to obtain salvation through our Lord Jesus Christ, who died for us so that whether we are awake or asleep we might live with him. Therefore encourage one another and build one another up, just as you are doing.
>
> 1 Thessalonians 5:4–11 ESV

- Paul reminds the Thessalonians that they are not children of the darkness, but children of the day. What do you think Paul is trying to do in these verses?
- Then Paul contrasts the lives and priorities of Christians with those in the surrounding community. What

stands out to you about these verses? In what ways do his words in these verses give courage?

- In the final sentence, Paul suggests that we build each other up in the way he had just been building up the Thessalonians: by reminding each other who we are in Christ. Why is this such a fundamental part of encouraging each other?

In his letter to the Galatian Christians, Paul speaks about sin and walking with each other through difficult and confusing times:

> Brothers and sisters, if someone is caught in a sin, you who live by the Spirit should restore that person gently. But watch yourselves, or you also may be tempted. Carry each other's burdens, and in this way you will fulfill the law of Christ.
>
> Galatians 6:1–2

- What do you notice about these verses? What do you think is Paul's main point?
- What do you think it means to restore someone gently after they've sinned? What does that sort of restoration look like? What does restoration without gentleness look like, and how is that counterproductive and un-Christlike?
- What do you think it means to "carry each other's burdens"?
- How does it give courage to others when you restore them after they've sinned?
- How does it give courage to carry someone's burden with them?

- Give one example of a time when you have given someone courage by bearing their burdens with them.

When people are going through a painful situation, it is critical to be a giver of courage. Part of that process is reminding each other of the truth. We have a wonderful example of this in 1 Thessalonians 4. The Thessalonian church was worried and discouraged because members of their congregation had died in Paul's absence. They wondered what would happen to someone who died before Jesus returned. Would they go to heaven? Paul wrote to reassure them, and encouraged them to be encouragers of each other in the same way:

> Brothers and sisters, we do not want you to be uninformed about those who sleep in death, so that you do not grieve like the rest of mankind, who have no hope. For we believe that Jesus died and rose again, and so we believe that God will bring with Jesus those who have fallen asleep in him. According to the Lord's word, we tell you that we who are still alive, who are left until the coming of the Lord, will certainly not precede those who have fallen asleep. For the Lord himself will come down from heaven, with a loud command, with the voice of the archangel and with the trumpet call of God, and the dead in Christ will rise first. After that, we who are still alive and are left will be caught up together with them in the clouds to meet the Lord in the air. And so we will be with the Lord forever. Therefore encourage one another with these words.
>
> 1 Thessalonians 4:13–18

- What do you notice about this passage? How did Paul give courage to the Thessalonians in the wake of tragedy?

- Paul does not tell the Thessalonians not to grieve; he says that because of Jesus they can grieve in a different manner—with hope. How does this idea give courage to those grieving a loss?
- Paul explicitly tells the Thessalonians to encourage each other with his words. Why do you think it is important to pass on to others encouragement that we have received from someone else?

Key Ideas in This Study

- To encourage is to give courage.
- To encourage is to call to one's side and provide comfort and reassurance.
- Encouragement includes reminding each other about our identities in Christ.
- Encouragement includes bearing each other's burdens.
- Encouragement includes restoring someone who has sinned.
- Encouragement includes reminding one another of the truth, especially in painful seasons.
- If we are encouraged, we are meant to pass that encouragement on to others.

Prayer

1. Starting with yourself, ask the group for two things:
   - A quick update on any ongoing prayer requests
   - New prayer requests

2. Write down the prayer requests as people share:

3. Ask someone in the group to close your meeting with prayer.

- **Sample prayer:** Lord Jesus, I want to be an encourager—a giver of courage. I want to be the type of person who calls others to my side and speaks life and truth and hope to them. I want to be a reminder of identity in Christ, a bearer of burdens, and a speaker of the truth. I want that to be my posture and my voice. I want to be willing to receive encouragement too. Please help me, Holy Spirit, to be a willing and effective encourager. Amen.

11

Judgmental No More

Social

A few questions to get your gathering started. This can be done during a meal or at the outset of your meeting.

- **Personal question:** Give us a quick snapshot of how things have been going since our last meeting—maybe a high and low point. (Everyone answers.)
- **Open-ended spiritual question:** What's something you feel God is teaching you right now? (A couple people share.)
- **Lead-in question to the subject of the study:** What do you think it means to judge others? What has been your experience of being judged? In what ways have you judged others?

Study

In the city where I live, there is a billboard on a prominent highway that reads, "Real Christians forgive like Jesus." I don't know who put this billboard in place, and I'm sure their motives were good, but there is a danger to this "real Christian" type of thinking. It teaches us a couple of things that are not biblical.

First, it teaches that our status as "real Christians" is based on our outwardly observable behavior. If we are not living up to Scripture's commands, then we are not real Christians. This flies in the face of the biblical gospel that teaches salvation by grace through faith in Christ. Are our actions important? Of course. Are we called to follow God's commands? Yes! But if we struggle to apply some of them in our lives, does that mean we are not genuine believers? No.

Second, this focus on identifying "real Christians" presumes that we are in a position to accurately evaluate whether someone else is a real Christian by what we observe in their life. This is not true either. We cannot see people's hearts; only God can.

When David was anointed king, God said this to Samuel:

> Do not consider his appearance or his height, for I have rejected him. The Lord does not look at the things people look at. People look at the outward appearance, but the Lord looks at the heart.
>
> 1 Samuel 16:7

When some first-century Jewish Christians were uncomfortable with gentiles being included in the Church without adhering to the Old Testament Law, Peter said this:

God, who knows the heart, showed that he accepted them by giving the Holy Spirit to them, just as he did to us. He did not discriminate between us and them, for he purified their hearts by faith.

Acts 15:8–9

God knows our hearts; we do not know each other's hearts. He is the only one in the position to make any determination about where we stand. When we try to evaluate the authenticity of someone else's faith based on what we observe, we actually preach a false gospel to ourselves: that our standing with God is based on how moral or pious we outwardly seem.

- What do you think about this "real Christian" line of thinking?
- What strikes you about the 1 Samuel and Acts 15 texts?
- Why do you think we judge each other so effortlessly?

Jesus warned us against the folly of judging others. In his famous Sermon on the Mount, Jesus said,

Do not judge, or you too will be judged. For in the same way you judge others, you will be judged, and with the measure you use, it will be measured to you. Why do you look at the speck of sawdust in your brother's eye and pay no attention to the plank in your own eye? How can you say to your brother, "Let me take the speck out of your eye," when all the time there is a plank in your own eye? You hypocrite, first take the plank out of your own eye, and then you will see clearly to remove the speck from your brother's eye.

Matthew 7:1–5

- What stands out to you about what Jesus said?
- What is the main reason that Jesus says we shouldn't judge?
- Why is removing the speck from your brother's eye (after having removed the plank from your own eye) not the same as judging someone?

In the Gospel of Luke, we discover a powerful parable that contrasts two people: one who seems outwardly pious (but is inwardly hard-hearted), and the other who seems outwardly sinful (but is inwardly righteous). In Luke 18 we read:

> To some who were confident of their own righteousness and looked down on everyone else, Jesus told this parable: "Two men went up to the temple to pray, one a Pharisee and the other a tax collector. The Pharisee stood by himself and prayed: 'God, I thank you that I am not like other people—robbers, evildoers, adulterers—or even like this tax collector. I fast twice a week and give a tenth of all I get.'
>
> "But the tax collector stood at a distance. He would not even look up to heaven, but beat his breast and said, 'God, have mercy on me, a sinner.'
>
> "I tell you that this man, rather than the other, went home justified before God. For all those who exalt themselves will be humbled, and those who humble themselves will be exalted."
>
> Luke 18:9–14

- Who is the audience of this parable?
- How would someone have described the Pharisee's spiritual life if all they knew was his outward behavior?
- How would someone have described the tax collector's spiritual condition based on his outward behavior?

- The term *justified* means to be declared innocent (i.e., acquitted from our sins/saved). Based on the parable, what was it about the tax collector that led him to be justified?
- What is the lesson about judging others from this parable?

Even though we are commanded not to judge each other, this does not mean that there is no judgment. Judgment is a biblical reality. Where we get confused is on the question of *who* is the judge. Scripture is clear that there is one judge, and it is God. As Paul put it:

> We must all appear before the judgment seat of Christ, so that each of us may receive what is due us for the things done while in the body, whether good or bad.
>
> 2 Corinthians 5:10

When the apostle Paul wrote to the Romans, he began by discussing the universal sinfulness of humanity in order to explain our common need for a savior. In Romans 2, he makes it very clear that we are not meant to judge each other:

> You, therefore, have no excuse, you who pass judgment on someone else, for at whatever point you judge another, you are condemning yourself, because you who pass judgment do the same things. Now we know that God's judgment against those who do such things is based on truth. So when you, a mere human being, pass judgment on them and yet do the same things, do you think you will escape God's judgment? Or do you show contempt for the riches of his kindness, forbearance

and patience, not realizing that God's kindness is intended to lead you to repentance?

Romans 2:1–4

- How does this relate to what Jesus said about judging in the Sermon on the Mount (Matthew 7:1–5)?
- What is the reason, according to Paul, that we should not judge others?
- What is Paul's point about God's judgment being based on truth?
- What is Paul's argument about God's kindness leading to repentance? What are we taking for granted when we judge others?

A little later in the same letter, Paul discusses the divisive issue of which foods Christians can eat together. He speaks to the fact that the Roman Christians were judging each other on this issue. Paul makes his case, alluding to the prophet Isaiah in the process:

You, then, why do you judge your brother or sister? Or why do you treat them with contempt? For we will all stand before God's judgment seat. It is written:

"'As surely as I live,' says the Lord, 'every knee will bow before me; every tongue will acknowledge God.'"

So then, each of us will give an account of ourselves to God.

Therefore let us stop passing judgment on one another. Instead, make up your mind not to put any stumbling block or obstacle in the way of a brother or sister.

Romans 14:10–13

- How does Paul's mention of the judgment seat compare to what he wrote in 2 Corinthians 5:10 (above)?
- What do you think about the idea of giving an account of yourself to God? How does this make you feel? Nervous? Comforted?
- Paul says that our focus should not be on judging each other; it should be on avoiding conflict and trying not to make things harder on each other. What do you think about this?

In Galatians, Paul contrasts life in the Spirit and life in the flesh. While this passage does not speak directly to the issue of judging, life in the flesh is characterized by attitudes and behaviors that lead to judgmentalism. Life in the Spirit leads to attitudes and behaviors that minimize judgmentalism. Paul writes,

So I say, walk by the Spirit, and you will not gratify the desires of the flesh. For the flesh desires what is contrary to the Spirit, and the Spirit what is contrary to the flesh. They are in conflict with each other, so that you are not to do whatever you want. But if you are led by the Spirit, you are not under the law.

The acts of the flesh are obvious: sexual immorality, impurity and debauchery; idolatry and witchcraft; hatred, discord, jealousy, fits of rage, selfish ambition, dissensions, factions and envy; drunkenness, orgies, and the like. I warn you, as I did before, that those who live like this will not inherit the kingdom of God.

But the fruit of the Spirit is love, joy, peace, forbearance, kindness, goodness, faithfulness, gentleness and self-control. Against such things there is no law. Those who belong to Christ Jesus have crucified the flesh with its passions and desires. Since we live by the Spirit, let us keep in step with the Spirit. Let us not become conceited, provoking and envying each other.

Galatians 5:16–26

- Of the qualities listed in the second paragraph, which lead to a judgmental attitude?
- Of the qualities listed in the third paragraph, which qualities help prevent a judgmental attitude?
- Envy was mentioned more than once in this passage. What do you believe is the relationship between envy and judging others?
- We are called to crucify our fleshly passions and desires. Judging others is one of them. What would it take for you to crucify your desire to pass judgment on others?

In his letter, James contrasts wisdom with envy and selfish ambition:

Who is wise and understanding among you? Let them show it by their good life, by deeds done in the humility that comes from wisdom. But if you harbor bitter envy and selfish ambition in your hearts, do not boast about it or deny the truth. Such "wisdom" does not come down from heaven but is earthly, unspiritual, demonic. For where you have envy and selfish ambition, there you find disorder and every evil practice.

But the wisdom that comes from heaven is first of all pure; then peace-loving, considerate, submissive, full of mercy and good fruit, impartial and sincere. Peacemakers who sow in peace reap a harvest of righteousness.

James 3:13–18

- What are some qualities that flow from wisdom?
- How do these qualities guard us against becoming judgmental?
- What are the dangers of envy and selfish ambition?

- How do envy and selfish ambition set us up to be judgmental people?

Much of our discussion in this chapter has been an argument in the negative: Don't judge. Don't embrace attitudes which lead to a judgmental or arrogant spirit. Let's close this chapter with an argument in the positive: Love each other. This is how we are meant to relate to one another instead of with judgmental attitudes. Paul wrote about this, most famously, in 1 Corinthians 13:

> If I speak in the tongues of men or of angels, but do not have love, I am only a resounding gong or a clanging cymbal. If I have the gift of prophecy and can fathom all mysteries and all knowledge, and if I have a faith that can move mountains, but do not have love, I am nothing. If I give all I possess to the poor and give over my body to hardship that I may boast, but do not have love, I gain nothing.
>
> Love is patient, love is kind. It does not envy, it does not boast, it is not proud. It does not dishonor others, it is not self-seeking, it is not easily angered, it keeps no record of wrongs. Love does not delight in evil but rejoices with the truth. It always protects, always trusts, always hopes, always perseveres.
>
> Love never fails.
>
> 1 Corinthians 13:1–8

- Paul essentially says, "I can speak the truth, but if I do so without love, I'm just making noise—not music." What do you think this means for our understanding of judging others?
- What is Paul's point in the rest of that paragraph?
- Of the characteristics of Christlike love detailed here, which stand out to you? Which help us to avoid

becoming judgmental, and how do they accomplish that?

Key Ideas in This Study

- God sees the heart; we do not.
- We preach a false gospel to ourselves when we evaluate others based on their outward behavior.
- To be judgmental is to be hypocritical.
- We will all stand before the judgment seat of Christ.
- Wisdom and humility will lead us away from judgmentalism. Envy and selfish ambition will lead us toward it.
- Showing Christlike love will help us avoid becoming judgmental.

Prayer

1. Starting with yourself, ask the group for two things:
   - A quick update on any ongoing prayer requests
   - New prayer requests

2. Write down the prayer requests as people share:

3. Ask someone in the group to close your meeting with prayer.

- **Sample prayer:** Heavenly Father, I know that I tend to judge others without seeing myself clearly. I know that I effortlessly notice others' faults while conveniently forgetting or minimizing my own. Help me not to judge. Help me to live life in the Spirit, not in the flesh. Help me to live a wise and humble life, not one characterized by envy and selfish ambition. Help me, Holy Spirit—knower of my heart—to grow in humility and Christlikeness. Soften my hardened and judgmental heart. Amen.

12

Sacrificial Sharers

Social

A few questions to get your gathering started. This can be done during a meal or at the outset of your meeting.

- **Personal question:** Give us a quick snapshot of how things have been going since our last meeting—maybe a high and low point. (Everyone answers.)
- **Open-ended spiritual question:** What's something you feel God is teaching you right now? (A couple people share.)
- **Lead-in question to the subject of the study:** When you think of sharing resources with others, do you consider this as being central to your faith? Why or why not?

Study

Sharing and generosity have been fundamental to Christian community from the beginning. While this might be evident from the New Testament, we in the modern Western world have an ambivalent view toward generosity and sharing with others. While most of us feel it is good or admirable to share with others, our individualistic, achievement-oriented culture can sometimes seem at odds with the biblical call to lift others up.

- In what ways do you feel the broader culture supports or undermines the biblical call to generosity and sharing?
- What is your basic view of what Christians are responsible to do in terms of taking care of those who are in need?

In the early days after Jesus's resurrection and ascension, we have clear evidence that the believers in Jerusalem supported the community of faith by sharing generously with each other.

They devoted themselves to the apostles' teaching and to fellowship, to the breaking of bread and to prayer. Everyone was filled with awe at the many wonders and signs performed by the apostles. All the believers were together and had everything in common. They sold property and possessions to give to anyone who had need. Every day they continued to meet together in the temple courts. They broke bread in their homes and ate together with glad and sincere hearts, praising God and enjoying the favor of all the people. And the Lord added to their number daily those who were being saved.

Acts 2:42–47

- What stands out to you about these verses?
- What do you find inspiring about this text?
- What do you find challenging?
- Are there portions of this passage that you find yourself having a knee-jerk negative reaction to? If so, which portions, and why do you think that is?

When the apostle Paul wrote to the Christians in Rome, he encouraged their generosity by doing two things: (1) highlighting the material needs of the relatively poor Christians in Judea and (2) pointing out how the churches in Greece had already made a financial contribution to help them.

> I hope to see you while passing through and to have you assist me on my journey [to Spain], after I have enjoyed your company for a while. Now, however, I am on my way to Jerusalem in the service of the Lord's people there. For Macedonia and Achaia were pleased to make a contribution for the poor among the Lord's people in Jerusalem. They were pleased to do it, and indeed they owe it to them. For if the Gentiles have shared in the Jews' spiritual blessings, they owe it to the Jews to share with them their material blessings. So after I have completed this task and have made sure that they have received this contribution, I will go to Spain and visit you on the way. I know that when I come to you, I will come in the full measure of the blessing of Christ.
>
> Romans 15:24–29

- How does Paul characterize his visit to Jerusalem?
- Macedonia and Achaia were regions in Greece. What was their attitude about giving?

- What is Paul's argument about the Jews sharing spiritually with the gentiles?
- What can we learn from what Paul told the Romans about generosity, and especially the *way* he encouraged them to give?

The churches in Greece served as an example to the Roman Christians. In Paul's second letter to the church in Corinth (one of the churches in Achaia), he encouraged them not to rest in their former generosity, but to follow through and continue to be generous. To do this, he used the churches in the north of Greece (Macedonia) as an example:

And now, brothers and sisters, we want you to know about the grace that God has given the Macedonian churches. In the midst of a very severe trial, their overflowing joy and their extreme poverty welled up in rich generosity. For I testify that they gave as much as they were able, and even beyond their ability. Entirely on their own, they urgently pleaded with us for the privilege of sharing in this service to the Lord's people. And they exceeded our expectations: They gave themselves first of all to the Lord, and then by the will of God also to us. So we urged Titus, just as he had earlier made a beginning, to bring also to completion this act of grace on your part. But since you excel in everything—in faith, in speech, in knowledge, in complete earnestness and in the love we have kindled in you—see that you also excel in this grace of giving.

I am not commanding you, but I want to test the sincerity of your love by comparing it with the earnestness of others. For you know the grace of our Lord Jesus Christ, that though he was rich, yet for your sake he became poor, so that you through his poverty might become rich.

And here is my judgment about what is best for you in this matter. Last year you were the first not only to give but also to have the desire to do so. Now finish the work, so that your eager willingness to do it may be matched by your completion of it, according to your means. For if the willingness is there, the gift is acceptable according to what one has, not according to what one does not have.

Our desire is not that others might be relieved while you are hard pressed, but that there might be equality.

2 Corinthians 8:1–13

- The Macedonian churches (Philippi, Thessalonica, and others) were generous in the midst of trials and even poverty. What example did they set for us?
- Paul says the Macedonian Christians gave on their own and viewed their financial gifts as a privilege. How does this attitude challenge us in our individualistic Western culture?
- Paul calls a financial gift an "act of grace." How is generous giving an act of God's grace?
- What is the reason that we are called to be generous?
- Paul encourages the Corinthians to follow through on their generous intentions. What seems to be going on here, and what is the lesson for us?
- What seems to be Paul's point in the last sentence?

The author of Hebrews speaks about generosity in terms of a sacrifice to God:

Through Jesus, therefore, let us continually offer to God a sacrifice of praise—the fruit of lips that openly profess his name. And do not forget to do good and to share with others, for with such sacrifices God is pleased.

Hebrews 13:15–16

- Praising God with our mouths is a sacrifice that pleases God. The author of Hebrews suggests that doing good and sharing with others is another form of sacrifice. In what ways is generous financial giving a sacrifice akin to an Old Testament temple sacrifice?

Giving, according to Paul, is an act of grace. Sharing financial resources with each other is a part of sharing and enjoying God's grace with each other. As Paul put it in Philippians,

> I thank my God every time I remember you. In all my prayers for all of you, I always pray with joy because of your partnership in the gospel from the first day until now, being confident of this, that he who began a good work in you will carry it on to completion until the day of Christ Jesus. It is right for me to feel this way about all of you, since I have you in my heart and, whether I am in chains or defending and confirming the gospel, all of you share in God's grace with me. God can testify how I long for all of you with the affection of Christ Jesus.
>
> Philippians 1:3–8

- The Philippians were partners with Paul in the gospel, sharing in God's grace with him. How does this relationship impact your view of sharing and generosity within your church?

Key Ideas in This Study

- Sharing and generosity have been fundamental to Christian community from the beginning.

- Wealthy Christians in the first century shared financial resources with poor Christians.
- Giving is a privilege.
- Giving is an act of grace.
- Giving must go beyond generous intentions; we must follow through.
- We give because Christ gave it all for us.
- Giving is a pleasing sacrifice to God.
- Sharing in God's grace includes financial giving.

Prayer

1. Starting with yourself, ask the group for two things:
   - A quick update on any ongoing prayer requests
   - New prayer requests

2. Write down the prayer requests as people share:

3. Ask someone in the group to close your meeting with prayer.

- **Sample prayer:** Lord Jesus, I want to be a generous person who follows through and actually shares what I have with those in need. I recognize that I tend to hoard the resources you've entrusted to me. Help me to give joyfully to my brothers and sisters in Christ within the Church. Prompt me, Holy Spirit, when you want me to meet a specific need. Help me to view the financial resources at my disposal as something to be managed in your name, rather than owned and used at my discretion. Shape my mind and heart on this issue. In Jesus's name, Amen.

13

Fellow Servants and Co-Heirs

Social

A few questions to get your gathering started. This can be done during a meal or at the outset of your meeting.

- **Personal question:** Give us a quick snapshot of how things have been going since our last meeting—maybe a high and low point. (Everyone answers.)
- **Open-ended spiritual question:** What's something you feel God is teaching you right now? (A couple people share.)
- **Lead-in question to the subject of the study:** When you think about fellow Christians—what are some words you would use to describe your relationship to them?

Study

In these last few chapters, we are going to drill deeper into the ancient language of the New Testament. We will explore some specific terms used by the New Testament authors to describe how Christians should think of and relate to each other within the Church. Taken together, these terms paint a rich picture of fellowship, mutual affection, and shared mission.

In the original language of the New Testament—ancient Greek—these terms we will explore all have the prefix *syn-*, which gives a word the connotation of being or doing something together with someone else. This *syn-* prefix made its way into English in words like *synergy*, which means to work together.

When encountering words like this in the New Testament, most biblical translators will translate them as *fellow (something)* or *co-(something)*, which brings out that feeling of togetherness. These words do not convey hierarchy and authority, but mutuality and common purpose.

In this chapter, we will explore instances of two *syn-* prefix Greek words in the New Testament, commonly translated as *fellow servant* and *fellow heir.**

Fellow Servant

In the New Testament letters, especially the letters of Paul, we get a glimpse of relationships within the early Church. There is, of course, theological content in the letters, but there is also a lot of relational content. Paul would mention specific people in the various churches around the Mediterranean, and in doing so, he would describe them. He would give us a sense

---

*The Greek word for *fellow servant* is σύνδουλος (*syndoulos*); *fellow heir* is συγκληρονόμος (*sygklēronomos*).

of their personal qualities and how they had served to advance the gospel. It is easy for us to skip over this personal content because it does not seem especially relevant to our lives today, but if we pay attention, we get glimpses of the beauty of Christian fellowship.

In his letter to the Colossians, Paul describes two people as *fellow servants*: Epaphras and Tychicus. Let's first read about what Paul has to say to the church in Colossae about Epaphras:

> We always thank God, the Father of our Lord Jesus Christ, when we pray for you, because we have heard of your faith in Christ Jesus and of the love you have for all God's people—the faith and love that spring from the hope stored up for you in heaven and about which you have already heard in the true message of the gospel that has come to you. In the same way, the gospel is bearing fruit and growing throughout the whole world—just as it has been doing among you since the day you heard it and truly understood God's grace. You learned it from Epaphras, our dear **fellow servant**, who is a faithful minister of Christ on our behalf, and who also told us of your love in the Spirit.
>
> Colossians 1:3–8

- What stood out to you about these verses at the beginning of the letter?
- How does Paul describe the Colossian church?
- What role did Epaphras play in the spiritual development of the church in Colossae?
- Why is it significant that the apostle Paul would refer to someone like Epaphras as his *fellow servant*?
- What other words did Paul use to describe Epaphras?

A little later in Paul's letter to the Colossians, he introduces Tychicus, who is also described as a fellow servant:

> Tychicus will tell you all the news about me. He is a dear brother, a faithful minister and **fellow servant** in the Lord. I am sending him to you for the express purpose that you may know about our circumstances and that he may encourage your hearts. He is coming with Onesimus, our faithful and dear brother, who is one of you. They will tell you everything that is happening here.
>
> Colossians 4:7–9

- How is Tychicus described by Paul?
- What seem to be some of the tasks assigned to Tychicus? Why are they important?
- How do you suppose the letter we call Colossians was delivered from Paul to the church in Colossae?
- Why is it important that we think of ourselves as servants?
- Why is it important that we think of each other as fellow servants, as Paul thought of Epaphras and Tychicus?
- How does thinking of ourselves and each other as servants promote health in the Church?

We are, therefore, servants. We serve Christ. We serve each other and we serve *with* each other. We serve those who don't know God. Thinking of ourselves and each other as servants is an important aspect of experiencing community in the Church. But, as God often does, he holds up two things to be true that seem contradictory. He is full of both grace *and* truth. He is a God of love *and* of justice.

In the same way, we are fellow servants of Christ, *and* we are also fellow heirs. *Servant* is a lowly term, implying that others are more important than we are. *Heir*, on the other hand, is a term of honor. But the New Testament teaches that both are true; we are fellow servants (as we saw above in the examples of Paul, Epaphras, and Tychicus), and we are also fellow heirs.

Fellow Heir

To be an heir is to be a child of someone with an inheritance to give. As we have already seen in this book, we enjoy fellowship with God as his children because of Jesus:

> See what great love the Father has lavished on us, that we should be called children of God! And that is what we are!
>
> 1 John 3:1

As God's children, we stand to inherit the blessings that come with being a part of his family. As Paul articulated in Romans 8, we are heirs:

> Those who are led by the Spirit of God are the children of God. The Spirit you received does not make you slaves, so that you live in fear again; rather, the Spirit you received brought about your adoption to sonship. And by him we cry, "Abba, Father." The Spirit himself testifies with our spirit that we are God's children. Now if we are children, then we are heirs—heirs of God and **co-heirs** with Christ, if indeed we share in his sufferings in order that we may also share in his glory.
>
> Romans 8:14–17

- What did you notice about these verses?
- *Abba* is an ancient Aramaic word that is roughly equivalent to "Da-da." It's an affectionate word used by a young child for his or her father. What does this tell you about your relationship with God through Christ?
- If we are God's children, Paul argues, then we are heirs. What do you think this means?
- What do you think it means that we—the Church—are co-heirs (or fellow heirs) with Christ? How should this affect our relationships with each other?
- This is a picture of simultaneously experiencing fellowship with each other and with Christ, as co-inheritors of the blessings that will come through God's kingdom. What does this make you feel about your spiritual life and your future?

In Ephesians, Paul brings out this idea of being fellow heirs when discussing how God has brought together Jews and gentiles in his Church:

> Surely you have heard about the administration of God's grace that was given to me for you, that is, the mystery made known to me by revelation, as I have already written briefly. In reading this, then, you will be able to understand my insight into the mystery of Christ, which was not made known to people in other generations as it has now been revealed by the Spirit to God's holy apostles and prophets. This mystery is that through the gospel the Gentiles are **heirs together** with Israel, members together of one body, and sharers together in the promise in Christ Jesus.
>
> Ephesians 3:2–6

- What stands out to you about this text?
- What is the "mystery" Paul is talking about?
- Why would it be surprising to Old Testament–era Israelites that one day the gentiles would be co-heirs with Israel in the Church?
- Jews and gentiles did not get along well in certain first-century congregations. What groups in the Church today might struggle with viewing each other as co-heirs? How can we help to bridge the divide?

In one of his letters, Peter speaks of husbands and wives as co-heirs together. In this text, Paul is encouraging husbands to view their wives as their spiritual equals—a radical perspective considering the patriarchal culture of the first-century Roman world:

Husbands, in the same way be considerate as you live with your wives, and treat them with respect as the weaker partner and as **heirs with you** of the gracious gift of life, so that nothing will hinder your prayers.

1 Peter 3:7

- Why is it important for husbands and wives to view each other as fellow heirs?
- How might a failure to do this hinder one's prayer life?

Key Ideas in This Study

- Paul called the people who served in his ministry fellow servants.

- We must think of ourselves as servants of Christ and consider each other fellow servants.
- We are simultaneously servants of Christ and children of God who are heirs to God's kingdom promises.
- Within the Church, we are co-heirs with people who are different from us.
- Husbands and wives should view each other as fellow heirs of God's promises.

Prayer

1. Starting with yourself, ask the group for two things:
   - A quick update on any ongoing prayer requests
   - New prayer requests

2. Write down the prayer requests as people share:

3. Ask someone in the group to close your meeting with prayer.

   - **Sample prayer:** Lord Jesus, help me to view myself in these terms that we have studied today. I want to view myself as a servant. I want to view my brothers and sisters in Christ as fellow servants, apart from any idea of hierarchy. I also, Lord, want to take seriously that you view me as your child and an heir of your kingdom promises! I want to have joy and confidence in that, and to view others in the Church as fellow heirs. I acknowledge that I am slow to think of myself as a servant, and quick to forget that you view me as a child. Help to shape my heart and mind along these lines. Amen.

14

Fellow Citizens and Soldiers

Social

A few questions to get your gathering started. This can be done during a meal or at the outset of your meeting.

- **Personal question:** Give us a quick snapshot of how things have been going since our last meeting—maybe a high and low point. (Everyone answers.)
- **Open-ended spiritual question:** What's something you feel God is teaching you right now? (A couple people share.)
- **Lead-in question to the subject of the study:** When you think back on your life, when did you feel the most camaraderie with another group of people? Maybe a group of co-workers or sports teammates? How would you describe the feeling of working side by side with them?

Study

Camaraderie is a powerful feeling, and one that cannot be experienced alone. A sense of shared mission and common purpose can encourage, inspire, and motivate us as we serve alongside others.

Two of the most potent forms of camaraderie are experienced through citizenship and military service. When we live in a particular nation or city, we feel a certain kinship with and concern for those who reside in the same locale. Rooting for the local sports team is an expression of this bond of citizenship: We support our sports team because they are engaged in a contest with other sports teams from cities that are not our home. Facing tragedies together can also bring out this bond of citizenship. For example, in my city of Houston, there was a palpable sense of camaraderie and solidarity when our city faced the catastrophe of Hurricane Harvey together.

Military service also creates a powerful sense of shared identity and mission. Men and women who have served and sacrificed together feel a deep bond with their fellow soldiers that can hardly be explained to those who were not serving with them.

According to the New Testament, Christians are also meant to experience camaraderie with each other as members of the body of Christ—the Church. We too are citizens and soldiers, though our hometown and the battles we're fighting are of a different nature.

In this chapter, we will continue to explore some specific words used by the New Testament authors to describe how followers of Christ should think of and relate to each other. As described in the previous chapter, these words—in the original Greek language of the New Testament—have the prefix *syn-*, which causes the word to mean doing something together *with* someone else. These words are typically translated as *fellow (something)* or *co-(something)*. Last chapter, we explored two terms translated as *fellow servant* and *fellow heir*.

We will now explore two more *syn-* prefix words that describe how Christians ought to view each other: *fellow citizen* and *fellow soldier*.*

Fellow Citizens

In his letter to the Philippians, Paul explains that our citizenship is not defined by earthly political boundaries:

> Our citizenship is in heaven. And we eagerly await a Savior from there, the Lord Jesus Christ, who, by the power that enables him to bring everything under his control, will transform our lowly bodies so that they will be like his glorious body.
>
> Philippians 3:20–21

- What do you think it means that our citizenship is in heaven?
- How do we balance the concept of our citizenship being in heaven with the call to be salt and light in the world now?

In the New Testament, there is one instance of the Greek word *sympolitēs*, translated into English as *fellow citizen*. It is found in chapter 2 of Paul's letter to the Ephesians. Let's explore the broader context of that word so that we can appreciate what Paul is saying:

---

*The Greek word for *fellow citizen* is συμπολίτης (*sympolitēs*); *fellow soldier* is συστρατιώτης (*systratiōtēs*).

Remember that formerly you who are Gentiles by birth and called "uncircumcised" by those who call themselves "the circumcision" (which is done in the body by human hands)—remember that at that time you were separate from Christ, excluded from citizenship in Israel and foreigners to the covenants of the promise, without hope and without God in the world. But now in Christ Jesus you who once were far away have been brought near by the blood of Christ.

Ephesians 2:11–13

Before Jesus, the gentiles (i.e., anyone who is not Jewish) were excluded from citizenship in Israel—God's people. Because of Christ, Paul states, those who were once far away have been brought near.

- How does Paul's language in these verses deepen your understanding of the gospel and your need for God?

In the next few verses, Paul describes how Jesus made a way for everyone to gain citizenship with God's people:

For he himself is our peace, who has made the two groups one and has destroyed the barrier, the dividing wall of hostility, by setting aside in his flesh the law with its commands and regulations. His purpose was to create in himself one new humanity out of the two, thus making peace, and in one body to reconcile both of them to God through the cross, by which he put to death their hostility. He came and preached peace to you who were far away and peace to those who were near. For through him we both have access to the Father by one Spirit.

Ephesians 2:14–18

- What stands out to you about these verses?
- What are some of the things Jesus did to make a way to offer citizenship to all who were far away from him?
- Are there any words you notice that are repeated in these verses? What do they tell you?

As a result of Jesus's work on the cross, Paul describes the new situation:

> Consequently, you are no longer foreigners and strangers, but **fellow citizens** with God's people and also members of his household, built on the foundation of the apostles and prophets, with Christ Jesus himself as the chief cornerstone.
>
> Ephesians 2:19–20

- Taking these verses and the preceding verses into account, what do you think it means to view brothers and sisters in Christ as fellow citizens?
- How does this perspective change your view of the Church?
- In what ways have you been a good citizen among God's people?
- In what ways can you be more Christlike toward fellow citizens of God's people?

Fellow Soldiers

The New Testament writers also describe Christians as fellow soldiers to each other. There are two instances of the word *systratiōtēs* in the New Testament, which we translate into English as *fellow soldier*. In both cases, they refer to work done by a specific individual serving under Paul's leadership. The first instance of *fellow soldier* is found in Philippians 2. Here, Paul is speaking directly to the church in Philippi:

> I think it is necessary to send back to you Epaphroditus, my brother, co-worker and **fellow soldier**, who is also your messenger, whom you sent to take care of my needs. For he longs for all of you and is distressed because you heard he was ill. Indeed he was ill, and almost died. But God had mercy on him, and not on him only but also on me, to spare me sorrow upon sorrow. Therefore I am all the more eager to send him, so that when you see him again you may be glad and I may have less anxiety. So then, welcome him in the Lord with great joy, and honor people like him, because he almost died for the work of Christ. He risked his life to make up for the help you yourselves could not give me.
>
> Philippians 2:25–30

- What struck you about these verses?
- What roles did Epaphroditus seem to play in the church at Philippi and in Paul's ministry?

The distance from Paul (imprisoned in Rome) to Philippi in northern Greece was hundreds of miles. It would have taken weeks or months for someone like Epaphroditus to carry letters between Paul and the Philippians.

- How does this information about travel—combined with what we read in Philippians—help to paint a picture of Epaphroditus as Paul's fellow soldier in the mission to share Christ with the world?

In the New Testament, the other instance of *fellow soldier* occurs at the beginning of Paul's letter to Philemon:

Paul, a prisoner of Christ Jesus, and Timothy our brother, to Philemon our dear friend and fellow worker—also to Apphia our sister and Archippus our **fellow soldier**—and to the church that meets in your home: Grace and peace to you from God our Father and the Lord Jesus Christ.

Philemon 1:1–3

Here, a man named Archippus is described as Paul's fellow soldier, but we do not get any more information about Archippus from this letter. But if we search his name, we find that Paul mentions Archippus—this fellow soldier—in the final two verses of another letter, Colossians:

Tell Archippus: "See to it that you complete the ministry you have received in the Lord." I, Paul, write this greeting in my own hand. Remember my chains. Grace be with you.

Colossians 4:17–18

Paul mentions Archippus in this letter to the Colossian church, and he also mentions Archippus in his letter to Philemon—which was also sent to the city of Colossae. So both mentions of Archippus are in letters destined for Colossae, which strongly suggests that Archippus must have lived in that city.

- What stands out to you about these two passages?
- What do you think it means when Paul said to Archippus, "See to it that you complete the ministry you have received in the Lord?"
- How might we view serving alongside each other in ministry as being fellow soldiers?

- Notice any similarities between what Paul said to Archippus and how he described Epaphroditus—another fellow soldier?
- What are some risks of thinking of brothers and sisters in Christ as fellow soldiers? How might we misunderstand this concept? What or whom are we fighting against?

Paul helps us to understand the battle we're fighting. In one of his letters to the Corinthian Christians, he wrote,

> Though we live in the world, we do not wage war as the world does. The weapons we fight with are not the weapons of the world.
>
> 2 Corinthians 10:3–4

Similarly, in Ephesians, Paul clarifies what he means when he talks about being engaged in a battle:

> Be strong in the Lord and in his mighty power. Put on the full armor of God, so that you can take your stand against the devil's schemes. For our struggle is not against flesh and blood, but against the rulers, against the authorities, against the powers of this dark world and against the spiritual forces of evil in the heavenly realms. Therefore put on the full armor of God, so that when the day of evil comes, you may be able to stand your ground, and after you have done everything, to stand. Stand firm then, with the belt of truth buckled around your waist, with the breastplate of righteousness in place, and with your feet fitted with the readiness that comes from the gospel of peace. In addition to all this, take up the shield of faith, with which you can extinguish all the flaming arrows of the evil one.

Take the helmet of salvation and the sword of the Spirit, which is the word of God.

Ephesians 6:10–17

- What do you think is the main point of Paul's words in these two passages?
- Whom are we fighting against?
- Whom are we *not* fighting against?
- What are the weapons we have at our disposal as fellow soldiers?

At the end of his life, Paul wrote these words about his life and ministry:

I am already being poured out like a drink offering, and the time for my departure is near. I have fought the good fight, I have finished the race, I have kept the faith.

2 Timothy 4:6–7

- What do you think it means to fight the good fight?
- What would you need to change about your life today in order to feel at the end of your life that you fought the good fight?

Key Ideas in This Study

- Christians are meant to experience camaraderie with each other as members of the body of Christ.
- Our citizenship is in heaven, and we should view brothers and sisters in Christ as fellow citizens.

- Paul called co-workers in ministry fellow soldiers.
- We do not wage war as the world does, and our weapons are not the weapons of the world.
- Our enemies are the spiritual forces that oppose Jesus.
- Our weapons are truth, the gospel, righteousness, faith, salvation, and the Word of God—all made available—and deployable—to us by the Spirit.
- We are fellow soldiers in a fight, and it is a good fight.

Prayer

1. Starting with yourself, ask the group for two things:
   - A quick update on any ongoing prayer requests
   - New prayer requests

2. Write down the prayer requests as people share:

3. Ask someone in the group to close your meeting with prayer.

   - **Sample prayer:** Lord Jesus, help me to view my brothers and sisters in Christ as fellow citizens of your people, and help me to view them also as fellow soldiers. Help me to desire and experience joy and camaraderie with them as I serve you, and help me to have a right view of my enemies. Help me to remember that people who do not know you are not my enemies; they are people you love and whom you wish to draw into relationship with you. Help me remember that my enemies are those spiritual forces who oppose you and your Church. Help me also to remember that your Spirit has equipped me with everything I need to fight the good fight alongside my fellow citizens and soldiers in the Church. Amen.

15

Fellow Workers

Social

A few questions to get your gathering started. This can be done during a meal or at the outset of your meeting.

- **Personal question:** Give us a quick snapshot of how things have been going since our last meeting—maybe a high and low point. (Everyone answers.)
- **Open-ended spiritual question:** What's something you feel God is teaching you right now? (A couple people share.)
- **Lead-in question to the subject of the study:** What makes someone a good co-worker or partner?

Study

On July 20, 1969, Neil Armstrong became the first human to set foot on the moon. In that historic moment, he uttered those unforgettable words: "That's one small step for a man, one giant leap for mankind."

Years later, when Armstrong was asked about those iconic phrases, he said that they were inspired by the hundreds of thousands of men and women who worked on the Apollo project and made his moment possible:

> I thought, "Well, when I step off . . . it's just going to be a little step." . . . But then I thought about all those 400,000 people that had given me the opportunity to make that step and thought, "It's going to be a big something for all those folks and indeed a lot of others that weren't even involved in the project." . . . It was a kind of simple correlation of thoughts.*

There is a unique feeling of satisfaction that comes from having worked alongside a team of people to accomplish something remarkable. Armstrong certainly isn't the only famous person to express these sentiments. We hear this kind of statement from other well-known people who achieve something special: Professional athletes thank their teammates after winning a championship. Actors who win awards typically thank the cast, the crew, and their families.

It's not just famous people who experience this feeling. Teachers celebrate a year completed with their fellow faculty members. Firefighters feel a sense of camaraderie with each other when they save a building or a life. Little League teams celebrate a winning season. Companies feel a sense of solidarity when they exceed a goal or invent something special. Parents feel this when they see a child begin to thrive as an adult.

---

*"Ed Bradley Talks to Neil Armstrong about Fame, Family and Apollo 11," *60 Minutes*, CBS, November 6, 2005.

- When have you experienced a sense of satisfaction in accomplishing something alongside co-workers or teammates?
- What makes an accomplishment like that so rewarding?

It might seem strange for the engineers or accountants at NASA to hear that Neil Armstrong considered them to be co-workers or partners in his work, because he seems like such a singular talent. But Armstrong did think of them as co-workers. Similarly, when we read the writings of the New Testament authors, we find that they considered their brothers and sisters in Christ to be partners and co-workers in their apostolic work.

In this session, we will explore another *syn-* word that is used thirteen times in the New Testament: *synergos*, often translated as *fellow worker* or *co-worker*.*

In the final chapter of Romans, the apostle Paul makes a number of personal remarks about friends and co-workers in ministry, and he uses this term *synergos* to describe them. Here are three examples:

> Greet Priscilla and Aquila, my **co-workers** in Christ Jesus. They risked their lives for me. Not only I but all the churches of the Gentiles are grateful to them. Greet also the church that meets at their house. . . . Greet Urbanus, our **co-worker** in Christ. . . . Timothy, my **co-worker**, sends his greetings to you.
>
> Romans 16:3–5, 9, 21

- What did you notice about these verses?
- What do we know about Priscilla and Aquila just from these verses, and how does it contribute to their status as Paul's co-workers?

*συνεργός (*synergos*).

136

- What is the significance of Paul calling Urbanus "our" co-worker instead of "my" co-worker?
- Why is it significant that Paul refers to those serving in his ministry as co-workers rather than as subordinates? What lesson can we learn from this practice?

As long as there have been leaders in the Church, there has been a comparison game happening. Leaders compare themselves with each other, and church members compare leaders with each other, choosing favorites. This has been a source of disunity for twenty centuries, and the apostle Paul tried to combat it in the first century. When the church in Corinth was comparing him with another leader, Apollos, Paul had this to say:

> When one says, "I follow Paul," and another, "I follow Apollos," are you not mere human beings? What, after all, is Apollos? And what is Paul? Only servants, through whom you came to believe—as the Lord has assigned to each his task. I planted the seed, Apollos watered it, but God has been making it grow. So neither the one who plants nor the one who waters is anything, but only God, who makes things grow. The one who plants and the one who waters have one purpose, and they will each be rewarded according to their own labor. For we are **co-workers** in God's service.
>
> 1 Corinthians 3:4–9

- What stands out to you about these verses?
- Apollos was probably viewed by many in the church to be a "rival" of Paul. Why is it noteworthy that Paul calls him a co-worker rather than asserting authority over Apollos?

- What is the reason Paul gives for thinking of others as co-workers rather than as subordinates?
- What lessons can we learn from this passage about our own lives and the Church today?

In 2 Corinthians, Paul is trying to repair a broken relationship with the Christians in Corinth. Paul had been contemplating a visit to Corinth to work things out, but he was very upset and so were they, so he sent a letter instead. In the first chapter, Paul wrote,

> I call God as my witness—and I stake my life on it—that it was in order to spare you that I did not return to Corinth. Not that we lord it over your faith, but **we work with you** for your joy, because it is by faith you stand firm.
>
> 2 Corinthians 1:23–24

- The phrase *we work with you for your joy* is more literally translated from the original Greek *we are co-workers of your joy*. Knowing that Paul is working for peace with the Corinthian church, how does it help him to refer to the Corinthians as co-workers?

In the same letter, Paul speaks of Titus, a trusted companion in the ministry who was instrumental in restoring the relationship between Paul and the Corinthians.

> As for Titus, he is my partner and **co-worker** among you; as for our brothers, they are representatives of the churches and an honor to Christ. Therefore show these men the proof of your love and the reason for our pride in you, so that the churches can see it.
>
> 2 Corinthians 8:23–24

- How would Paul calling Titus his co-worker help Titus in his mission to smooth things over with the Corinthians? How might Titus be treated differently if Paul referred to him as a subordinate?

Epaphroditus was another of Paul's co-workers. Paul labeled him that way in Philippians 2:

> I think it is necessary to send back to you Epaphroditus, my brother, **co-worker** and fellow soldier, who is also your messenger, whom you sent to take care of my needs. For he longs for all of you and is distressed because you heard he was ill. Indeed he was ill, and almost died. But God had mercy on him, and not on him only but also on me, to spare me sorrow upon sorrow. Therefore I am all the more eager to send him, so that when you see him again you may be glad and I may have less anxiety. So then, welcome him in the Lord with great joy, and honor people like him, because he almost died for the work of Christ. He risked his life to make up for the help you yourselves could not give me.
>
> Philippians 2:25–30

- In what ways did Epaphroditus help Paul to lead and take care of the church in Philippi?

In Philippians 4, Paul—as he did in 2 Corinthians—referred to people in conflict as co-workers:

> Therefore, my brothers and sisters, you whom I love and long for, my joy and crown, stand firm in the Lord in this way, dear friends! I plead with Euodia and I plead with Syntyche to be of the same mind in the Lord. Yes, and I ask you, my true companion, help these women since they have contended at my side in

the cause of the gospel, along with Clement and the rest of my **co-workers**, whose names are in the book of life.

Philippians 4:1–3

- Here, Paul describes disunity in the church and specific people who are at odds. How might calling them co-workers help them desire peace with each other?

In Colossians 4, Paul mentions specific people in his ministry and reveals that he has been comforted by these co-workers:

My fellow prisoner Aristarchus sends you his greetings, as does Mark, the cousin of Barnabas. (You have received instructions about him; if he comes to you, welcome him.) Jesus, who is called Justus, also sends greetings. These are the only Jews among my **co-workers** for the kingdom of God, and they have proved a comfort to me.

Colossians 4:10–11

- How is it comforting to feel that you are in the trenches working alongside someone?
- Why is it important to know that our leaders need the support and comfort of their co-workers?

When the Thessalonian Christians were experiencing persecution and social antagonism, Paul sent Timothy to comfort them:

When we could stand it no longer, we thought it best to be left by ourselves in Athens. We sent Timothy, who is our brother and **co-worker** in God's service in spreading the gospel of Christ, to strengthen and encourage you in your faith, so that no one would be unsettled by these trials. For you know quite well that we are destined for them. In fact, when we were with you, we kept telling you that we would be persecuted. And it turned out that way, as you well know. For this reason, when I could stand it no longer, I sent to find out about your faith. I was afraid that in some way the tempter had tempted you and that our labors might have been in vain.

1 Thessalonians 3:1–5

- What stands out to you about this passage?
- How is Timothy described?
- What was Timothy's role with the Thessalonians during the difficult time they were experiencing?

At the beginning and ending of Paul's letter to Philemon, he spoke of his co-workers:

Paul, a prisoner of Christ Jesus, and Timothy our brother, to Philemon our dear friend and **fellow worker**. . . . Epaphras, my fellow prisoner in Christ Jesus, sends you greetings. And so do Mark, Aristarchus, Demas and Luke, **my fellow workers**.

Philemon 1:1, 23–24

- What stands out to you about these verses?
- Paul sends this letter to a fellow worker, and sends greetings to that fellow worker from other fellow workers. What picture does this paint for you of the early Church?

In one of his letters, Jesus's disciple John connects Christian hospitality to working together:

Dear friend, you are faithful in what you are doing for the brothers and sisters, even though they are strangers to you. They have told the church about your love. Please send them on their way in a manner that honors God. It was for the sake of the Name that they went out, receiving no help from the pagans. We ought therefore to show hospitality to such people so that we may **work together** for the truth.

3 John 1:5–8

- What seems to be happening in these verses?
- What is the connection between hospitality and serving together in ministry?

Key Ideas in This Study

- The first-century Church leaders spoke of their friends in ministry as co-workers.
- Referring to each other—and treating each other—as co-workers can help in peacemaking processes.
- Leaders thinking of other leaders as co-workers cultivates humility and minimizes disunity in the Church.
- Working together with others is comforting and encouraging.

Prayer

1. Starting with yourself, ask the group for two things:
   - A quick update on any ongoing prayer requests
   - New prayer requests

2. Write down the prayer requests as people share:

3. Ask someone in the group to close your meeting with prayer.

- **Sample prayer:** Lord Jesus, I want to be a co-worker in your kingdom alongside my brothers and sisters in Christ. I realize that I have a tendency to either elevate myself or think too little of my contributions. Help me to have the perspective of Paul and the other New Testament authors, who thought of themselves and others as co-workers. Amen.

16

Fellow Prisoners and Co-Sufferers

Social

A few questions to get your gathering started. This can be done during a meal or at the outset of your meeting.

- **Personal question:** Give us a quick snapshot of how things have been going since our last meeting—maybe a high and low point. (Everyone answers.)
- **Open-ended spiritual question:** What's something you feel God is teaching you right now? (A couple people share.)
- **Lead-in question to the subject of the study:** What do you think it means to suffer with someone?

Study

In this chapter, we will explore one more word used by the New Testament authors to describe how followers of Christ should think of and relate to each other. As discussed in previous chapters, these words—in the original Greek language of the New Testament—have the prefix *syn-*, which causes the word to mean doing something together *with* someone else. These words are typically translated as *fellow (something)* or *co-(something)*.

In this chapter we will explore the term *fellow prisoner* and the broader concept of brothers and sisters in Christ suffering with each other.*

In the middle of the first century, as Christianity began to spread out through the Roman world and permeate into both urban and rural areas, there began to exist a social friction between Christians and their pagan neighbors. Sometimes that friction caught the attention of the civil or imperial authorities, which resulted in the imprisonment or martyrdom of first-century Christians. The belief in Jesus as God's Son—the one true Lord and Savior—was viewed as blasphemous, treasonous, or at least unpatriotic in many communities because Roman propaganda taught that Caesar was the divine lord and savior.†

---

*The Greek term for *fellow prisoner* in the New Testament is συναιχμάλωτος (*synaichmalōtos*).

†In the early second century, a Roman governor named Pliny corresponded with the Roman emperor Trajan about how he should go about arresting, interrogating, and punishing Christians. He wondered whether it was a crime merely to *be* a Christian, or if punishment should be based on certain actions. The emperor replied by suggesting that Christians could prove their innocence by making sacrifices to the Greco-Roman deities and, presumably, himself. (Pliny, *Letters*, 10.96–97.)

This persecution was not a surprise to the earliest follow-ers of Christ. Jesus himself had prepared his disciples for this reality:

> Be on your guard; you will be handed over to the local councils and be flogged in the synagogues. On my account you will be brought before governors and kings as witnesses to them and to the Gentiles. But when they arrest you, do not worry about what to say or how to say it. At that time you will be given what to say, for it will not be you speaking, but the Spirit of your Father speaking through you.
>
> Matthew 10:17–20

- What stands out to you about these verses?
- Have you ever experienced antagonism or bullying be-cause of your faith in Christ? If so, how did you sense God leading you through that experience?

Similarly, when Jesus spoke about discipleship, he spoke about it in terms of a willingness to suffer. This is central to what it means to be a Christian. It does not mean that each of us *will* suffer direct persecution, but we must be *willing* to do so. As Jesus put it:

> Whoever wants to be my disciple must deny themselves and take up their cross and follow me. For whoever wants to save their life will lose it, but whoever loses their life for me will find it.
>
> Matthew 16:24–25

- How do these verses strike you?
- What do you think most Westerners think when they read these words?

- What do you think it means to take up our cross?
- Why is it hard for us to remember (and embrace) that a willingness to suffer is part of the call of discipleship?

Jesus addressed the same concept in John 15. When speaking to his disciples on the eve of his arrest, he said:

> If the world hates you, keep in mind that it hated me first. If you belonged to the world, it would love you as its own. As it is, you do not belong to the world, but I have chosen you out of the world. That is why the world hates you. Remember what I told you: "A servant is not greater than his master." If they persecuted me, they will persecute you also.
>
> John 15:18–20

- Do you find it discouraging or encouraging to know that followers of Jesus will experience various forms of suffering as Jesus did?

As chronicled in the book of Acts, first-century Christians faced imprisonment for their faith.* The apostle Paul was imprisoned on several occasions for his evangelistic activity, and in his letters he used the term *fellow prisoner* to refer to several of his co-workers in ministry who experienced the same thing:

> Epaphras, my **fellow prisoner** in Christ Jesus, sends you greetings.
>
> Philemon 1:23

*See Acts 8:3; 12:4–17; 16:23–40; 20:23; 22:4; 24:27; 26:10.

My **fellow prisoner** Aristarchus sends you his greetings, as does Mark, the cousin of Barnabas.

Colossians 4:10

Greet Andronicus and Junia, my fellow Jews **who have been in prison with me.** They are outstanding among the apostles, and they were in Christ before I was.

Romans 16:7

- What do you notice about these three texts?
- What are the names of Paul's fellow prisoners listed in these texts?
- Have you noticed these mentions of Paul's fellow prisoners before? Why do you think it's easy to miss details like this when reading Paul's letters?
- In what ways do you think Paul's ministry might have been deepened and enhanced by his time in prison? (Read Philippians 1:12–14 for one example.)
- If you were imprisoned because you are a Christian, how do you think you would respond? How would it affect your faith in God?
- Today, there are thousands of Christians around the world experiencing imprisonment (or worse) for their faith. In what ways might you support them?

It was a literal, historical reality that Paul spent time in prison with other believers. He suffered, incarcerated, alongside them. This is just one example of the broader call for members of the Church to be willing to suffer with each other. Consider the words of the author of Hebrews:

Keep on loving one another as brothers and sisters. Do not forget to show hospitality to strangers, for by so doing some people have shown hospitality to angels without knowing it. Continue to remember those in prison **as if you were together with them in prison,** and those who are mistreated as if you yourselves were suffering.

Hebrews 13:1–3*

- How is remembering those in prison an example of loving someone as a brother or sister in Christ?
- How might it look for you to remember those in prison so deeply and consistently that it's as if you yourself were with them?
- Who do you know who has suffered for their faith, and how can you walk with them through the difficulties they have faced?

A willingness to suffer with each other is at the heart of what it means to be the Church. We are meant to care about each other so deeply—we are called to be so unified as a part of the body of Christ—that we cannot help but suffer alongside each other and feel pain with those who feel pain. It is meant to be an instinctive response to suffer with those who are suffering. Paul spoke about this reality in 1 Corinthians 12:

The eye cannot say to the hand, "I don't need you!" And the head cannot say to the feet, "I don't need you!" On the contrary, those parts of the body that seem to be weaker are indispensable, and the parts that we think are less honorable we treat with special honor. And the parts that are unpresentable are treated with special modesty, while our presentable parts need no special treatment. But God has put the body together, giving

---

*In Hebrews 13:3, the author uses a different Greek word for *fellow prisoner* (συνδέω /*syndeō*).

greater honor to the parts that lacked it, so that there should be no division in the body, but that its parts should have equal concern for each other. If one part suffers, every part suffers with it; if one part is honored, every part rejoices with it.

1 Corinthians 12:21–26

- What do you notice about this text?
- What does it mean for members of the Church to have "equal concern for each other"? Why is this so challenging?
- How can Christians in the Western world, who generally do not face violent persecution, stand with and suffer with those in other parts of the world where Christians face physical danger?
- How can we cultivate an awareness of what God is doing in his Church around the globe, so that we can suffer and celebrate with our brothers and sisters in the body of Christ?

When Jesus's disciple Peter wrote a letter to a congregation that was experiencing pain and suffering, he spoke about the call to suffer and how we should respond to antagonism and persecution that come our way:

Dear friends, do not be surprised at the fiery ordeal that has come on you to test you, as though something strange were happening to you. But rejoice inasmuch as you participate in the sufferings of Christ, so that you may be overjoyed when his glory is revealed. If you are insulted because of the name of Christ, you are blessed, for the Spirit of glory and of God rests on you. If you suffer, it should not be as a murderer or thief or any other kind of criminal, or even as a meddler. However, if you suffer as a Christian, do not be ashamed, but praise God that you bear that name.

1 Peter 4:12–16

- What did you notice about these verses?
- Peter suggests that it is not strange to have a "fiery ordeal" come our way as followers of Christ. Why do we often feel that suffering for our faith is strange or out of the ordinary?
- What do you think about Peter's words that we can experience joy by participating in the sufferings of Christ? Or when he said that we are blessed when we are insulted?
- Peter makes a distinction between deserved suffering (for committing a crime) and undeserved suffering (for being a Christian). He suggests that we should not feel shame for suffering for our faith. Why do you think it is easy to feel ashamed if we are mistreated for following Jesus?

Key Ideas in This Study

- Jesus told us to expect suffering for following him and called us to be willing to take up our crosses.
- Paul and many other first-century Christians spent time in prison for their faith.
- We are called to love each other as brothers and sisters, which means a willingness to suffer with each other.
- Persecution or antagonism for our faith should not be seen as strange or surprising.

- We can experience a unique type of joy by suffering for our faith.

Prayer

1. Starting with yourself, ask the group for two things:
   - A quick update on any ongoing prayer requests
   - New prayer requests

2. Write down the prayer requests as people share:

3. Ask someone in the group to close your meeting with prayer.

   - **Sample prayer:** Lord Jesus, I understand that you call me to be willing to suffer in your name. I confess that I don't often think of suffering as part of my faith life. I usually do not heed the call to suffer with others who are suffering. In fact, I spend much of my life avoiding pain. Help me, Lord, to be willing to truly take up my cross and be open to whatever you have for me—even if it is a form of suffering. I want to experience the unique joy of participating in your sufferings. Grow my heart and mind in this area, and give me courage. Amen.

Conclusion

Being the Church

The Church is a truly unique entity. It is beyond compare. It is not limited by time or geography. It is not a corporation. It is not a nation-state or political affiliation. It is not a philanthropic group. It is not an event to be attended. It is not an impersonal organization. It is not a physical structure.

The very language of the New Testament proves this. The ancient Greek term we translate as *Church* is ἐκκλησία (*ekklēsia*), which refers to a gathering or assembly of people—literally "those called out." This leads us to an important biblical insight that we have glimpsed in the preceding chapters, but that we must say now explicitly:

> **We Christians don't *go to* church;**
> **we Christians *are* the Church.**

This means that how we think about and act toward others really counts. Personal relationships in the Church are not peripheral concerns to be managed; the Church is, by nature and design, relational. The experience of *koinōnia* with God and each other is at the very heart of what it means to be a Christian.

The Church is the body of Christ, an eternal, spiritual organism made up of people transformed by Christ into new creations. As a result of Jesus's work on the cross, we have been invited into this true, life-giving *koinōnia* with God and one another. This precious and costly invitation has been extended to us not because of any merit on our part; it is wholly a gift of God's grace. The Church is the pillar and foundation of truth in our lives and in our world, and in the Church we are invited to enjoy—together—the life that is truly life.

But we do not always experience it that way. Even though we are not ruled by sin anymore—as Paul eloquently articulated in Romans 6—we still do sin. Sometimes unknowingly. Sometimes accidentally. Sometimes intentionally. This means that Christians regularly behave toward each other (and the rest of the world) in ways that are not Christlike.

In addition to this daily friction caused by sin, it seems to me that many of the frustrations within the Church flow from two fundamental misunderstandings:

1. We forget who oversees the Church.
2. We try to be the Church in our own strength.

Who Oversees the Church?

In Colossians 1, Paul wrote down what many biblical scholars believe is a first-century Christian hymn. Paul may have authored the hymn, or he may have simply recorded the words to a song that early Christians were singing in their worship gatherings. Regardless, it is one of the most ancient expressions of Jesus's nature:

> The Son is the image of the invisible God, the firstborn over all creation. For in him all things were created: things in heaven and on earth, visible and invisible, whether thrones or powers or rulers or authorities; all things have been created through him and for him. He is before all things, and in him all things hold together. And he is the head of the body, the church; he is the beginning and the firstborn from among the dead, so that in everything he might have the supremacy. For God was pleased to have all his fullness dwell in him, and through him to reconcile to himself all things, whether things on earth or things in heaven, by making peace through his blood, shed on the cross.
>
> Colossians 1:15–20

While the song-like qualities are not readily observable in the English translation, the meaning of the rich lyrics is clear: Christ is the eternal creator—God in the flesh. He is the head of the Church and has offered peace and reconciliation through his work on the cross.

Jesus is the head of the Church. He is a leader without peer. He is both our example of a God-honoring life, and our source of strength for living that life. When we try to take the reins and remake the Church in our own image, we become embroiled in a myriad of distractions, divisions, and foolish controversies. If we are going to enjoy genuine *koinōnia* as the body of Christ, we must acknowledge that Christ is the head of the Church and trust him to lead us.

But how can we do this?

How Can We Be the Church That Christ Calls Us to Be?

As we have seen in the prior chapters, Christians are called to think and act in ways that honor Christ, build up the Church, and reflect Christlikeness to the world. We are called to be generous, humble, hospitable, and selfless. We are commanded to put each other first and edify one another. In our own strength, these actions and attitudes are not merely difficult; they are impossible. We cannot power the Church and our personal spiritual growth on our own. We must trust and rely on God to work in and through us. As Jesus said,

> Remain in me, as I also remain in you. No branch can bear fruit by itself; it must remain in the vine. Neither can you bear fruit unless you remain in me. "I am the vine; you are the branches. If you remain in me and I in you, you will bear much fruit; apart from me you can do nothing."
>
> John 15:4–5

If we are to live a life worthy of our calling, if we are to be the Church we are called to be, we must remain in Christ. Jesus was clear: We cannot bear fruit on our own. But he promised that we would not be alone; he would send his Spirit to enable us to live a Christlike life as a part of his Church:

> The Advocate, the Holy Spirit, whom the Father will send in my name, will teach you all things and will remind you of everything I have said to you.
>
> John 14:26

You will receive power when the Holy Spirit comes on you; and you will be my witnesses in Jerusalem, and in all Judea and Samaria, and to the ends of the earth.

Acts 1:8

The church throughout Judea, Galilee and Samaria enjoyed a time of peace and was strengthened. Living in the fear of the Lord and encouraged by the Holy Spirit, it increased in numbers.

Acts 9:31

The Spirit lives within us, and he knows our hearts. As we yield our lives more and more to him, he will strengthen our hearts and grow us in Christlikeness. He will give us courage and shape us into givers of courage. He will enable us to enjoy *koinōnia* with our brothers and sisters in Christ, to live lives as servants and heirs, citizens and soldiers, co-sufferers and fellow workers. And as we experience this fellowship within the Church, the Spirit will work through us to change lives in our communities and in our families.

Christian fellowship is beautiful, but it is not always easy. We must remember that Jesus is the head of the Church, and the Holy Spirit is the one who enables us to honor the Lord, reflect Christ to the world, and enjoy fellowship with each other.

My parting prayer is that you would open up your heart to the Lord in a fresh way and experience *koinōnia* with him and others like never before. As the apostle Paul put it:

May the God of hope fill you with all joy and peace as you trust in him, so that you may overflow with hope by the power of the Holy Spirit.

Romans 15:13

Ryan Lokkesmoe is the lead pastor of Real Hope Community Church in the Houston area. As an undergrad, he studied criminal justice before going on to earn his MA in New Testament at Gordon-Conwell Theological Seminary and his PhD in New Testament at the University of Denver. His doctoral work focused on the historical context of first-century Christianity.

Ryan previously served as the small-groups pastor of a large multisite church, personally consulted with ministry leaders from around the country about small groups, and developed small-group curriculum for LifeWay. Ryan is the author of *Blurry: Bringing Clarity to the Bible* and *Paul and His Team: What the Early Church Can Teach Us about Leadership and Influence* and also teaches biblical studies at a local seminary.

Ryan loves music and books and is both a history buff and a close follower of current events. But most of all, he loves spending time with his wife and their two children.

More from
Ryan Lokkesmoe

Starting a small group can be intimidating, but pastor Ryan Lokkesmoe gives you the tools to lead effectively. This down-to-earth resource focuses on practical pointers and overcoming challenges, and provides tips on leading discussions. The book also includes sample Bible studies and topical studies with icebreakers, discussion questions, and guides for leading prayer times.

Small Groups Made Easy

BETHANYHOUSE